Everyday Investing: A Practical Guide to Personal Financial Growth

Joey Amato

PRAISE FOR EVERYDAY INVESTING

"I can't thank Joey enough for writing 'Everyday Investing'. As someone who was always intimidated by the world of finance, this book has been a game-changer for me. The author's ability to simplify complex investment concepts and make them accessible to anyone is truly remarkable.
What sets this book apart is its holistic approach to personal investing. It doesn't just focus on the numbers and strategies; it delves into the emotional aspects of investing and helps readers overcome common pitfalls. The insights on aligning personal values with investment choices opened my eyes to the power of socially responsible investing, allowing me to invest with purpose.
'Everyday Investing' is more than just a guide; it's a roadmap to financial freedom and empowerment. The practical examples and guidance provided throughout the book have given me the confidence to take charge of my financial future. I now have a personalized investment plan that aligns with my goals and aspirations." – Daniel B. / Los Angeles, CA

"As someone who has always felt overwhelmed by the world of investing, 'Everyday Investing' has been a lifesaver.
I cannot recommend this book enough. Whether you're a novice or have some investment experience, 'Everyday Investing' is a must-read. It's an invaluable resource that will transform your mindset, empower you to make informed decisions, and set you on a path towards financial success." – Shelby, J / New York City, NY

"I absolutely loved reading 'Everyday Investing'. This book has truly changed the way I approach my finances and investing. With clear and concise explanations, Joey has made investing accessible to anyone, regardless of their financial background.
The author's emphasis on ongoing education and adaptation in the investment world is invaluable. The book provides a wealth of resources and tools to stay ahead of market trends and make sound investment decisions. It's not just a one-time read; it's a reference guide that I keep coming back to whenever I need a refresher or want to explore new strategies.
If you're looking for a comprehensive guide that will transform your understanding of personal finance and investing, look no further." – Shawn W. / Chicago, IL

Introduction

Welcome to the exciting world of personal investing! In this book, we will embark on a journey that will transform your understanding of money, empower you to take control of your financial future, and guide you on the path to achieving your goals.

Investing is not just for the wealthy or the financial gurus. It is a powerful tool that can help individuals from all walks of life build wealth, secure their financial well-being, and unlock a world of possibilities. Whether you are starting with a small amount or have significant funds to invest, this book is designed to provide you with the knowledge, strategies, and confidence to make informed investment decisions.

The realm of personal investing can sometimes appear daunting, filled with complex terminology, market fluctuations, and a seemingly endless array of options. But fear not! We will navigate through the maze of investment concepts, demystify jargon, and present information in a clear and accessible manner.

This book is not just about numbers and charts; it is about your aspirations, dreams, and the future you envision. It is about understanding your personal financial goals, defining what truly matters to you, and devising a personalized investment plan to bring those goals to fruition.

Throughout this book, we will cover a wide range of topics, starting with the basics of investing and gradually diving into more advanced concepts. We will explore various investment vehicles, such as stocks, bonds, mutual funds, and real estate, understanding their characteristics, risks, and potential rewards. We will delve into the importance of diversification, asset allocation, and risk management strategies to safeguard your investments.

But investing is not just about numbers; it is about aligning your financial decisions with your values and aspirations. We will explore the impact of your personal values on investment choices, including socially responsible investing and sustainable investing.

Moreover, we will discuss the role of emotions in investing, as well as common pitfalls to avoid. We will equip you with the tools to overcome fear, greed, and other emotional biases that can derail your investment journey. Additionally, we will address the importance of ongoing education, adapting to market changes, and staying informed in the ever-evolving investment landscape.

Some principles and concepts are mentioned numerous times throughout this book. I did this purposefully for two reasons. First, to stress the importance of the concept and second, so you can learn its meaning and ingrain it in your memory. Studies have shown that you need to read something a few times to remember if fully.

By the time you reach the final page of this book, you will have gained a solid foundation in personal investing and be well-prepared to take charge of your financial destiny. Remember, investing is a lifelong journey, and each step you take brings you closer to your goals. So, let's embark on this adventure together, embracing the power of personal investing and unlocking a world of financial opportunities.

ABOUT ME

Let me tell you a bit about myself and why you should take my advice. When I was 29 years of age, I was over $50,000 in debt. I had the fortune of having parents who paid for my college education, so this debt was solely from credit card use. I was living in Orlando and had made friends with a wonderful group of people who just happened to be older than myself and extremely wealthy. To fit in, I dined at fancy restaurants, drank expensive lattes twice a day, and shopped at designer boutiques. I didn't realize it costs money to try to be rich.

Before I knew it, I was shoulder deep in debt and couldn't find a way to claw myself out of it until I grabbed hold of my financial life and stopped trying to keep up with the Joneses. I cut things out, scaled back on dining out all the time, and started shopping at discount retailers for clothes. Slowly, I began paying off some of the credit cards starting with the highest interest-rate cards first, then moving to the card with the next highest rate.

In less than a decade, not only did all of my cards get paid off, but I had a positive net worth for the first time. Things were finally starting to look up. As my income began to grow, I began investing. A thousand dollars here. A thousand dollars there. Before I knew it, I had amassed a few hundred thousand dollars, thanks in part to some great stock market returns. Funny enough, my greatest returns were on stocks that most people would consider boring. Not the tech names that get all of the attention.

As I write this book, I am 42 years old and on the verge of being able to retire. I don't have Elon Musk money in the bank, but I have enough to retire and live comfortably *if* I want to. I own my home in Indianapolis, am 2 years away from paying off my car, and have less than $500 in credit card debt – which I pay off each month.

If I can do it, you can do it. I have learned so much throughout my investment journey, I want to pass on this knowledge to you. I hope you enjoy this book and begin investing today. Whether it's $10, $100, or $1,000, invest something now.

Money + Time = Financial Freedom!

CONTENTS

CHAPTER ONE

The Importance of Investing for Long-Term Financial Security

Securing long-term financial stability is crucial in today's fast-paced and ever-changing world. One of the most effective ways to achieve this is through investing. Investing is not just for the wealthy or financial experts; it is a powerful tool that individuals of all income levels can utilize to grow their wealth over time. Below, we will explore the importance of investing for long-term financial security and how it can positively impact your future.

Building Wealth and Beating Inflation:

Investing allows your money to work for you by generating returns and compounding over time. By allocating your funds to various asset classes, such as stocks, bonds, real estate, or mutual funds, you have the potential to grow your wealth exponentially. This growth surpasses the rate of inflation, ensuring that your money maintains its purchasing power and preserves your financial security.

Retirement Planning:

Investing is particularly crucial for retirement planning. Depending solely on traditional savings accounts or relying on pension plans may not be sufficient to sustain your desired lifestyle during retirement. By investing in retirement accounts like 401(k)s, IRAs, or personal investment portfolios, you can accumulate a substantial nest egg that will support you throughout your golden years. The power of compounding and long-term investment growth can significantly enhance your retirement savings and provide peace of mind.

Diversification and Risk Management:

Investing allows you to diversify your portfolio by spreading your investments across various asset classes, industries, and geographic regions. Diversification helps mitigate risks by reducing the impact of individual investment failures. By not putting all your eggs in one basket, you can potentially protect your investments from market volatility and economic downturns. Maintaining a balanced portfolio with a mix of low-risk and higher-risk investments aligns with your risk tolerance and ensures a smoother financial journey.

Capitalizing on Market Opportunities:

Financial markets are constantly evolving and present numerous investment opportunities. You can benefit from economic growth and technological advancements by participating in the market. Investing in promising companies or sectors can yield substantial returns over time. While there are inherent risks, thorough research and a long-term perspective can help you identify opportunities that align with your investment goals and risk tolerance.

Beating the Erosion of Purchasing Power:

Keeping your money idle in low-interest savings accounts or under the mattress means losing out on potential gains. Inflation erodes the value of your money over time, making it essential to invest in assets that can outpace inflation. By investing wisely, you not only preserve your purchasing power but also have the opportunity to generate substantial returns that exceed the inflation rate.

Flexibility and Financial Freedom:

Investing provides you with financial flexibility and freedom to pursue your goals and aspirations. Whether it's starting a business, funding your children's education, or taking that dream vacation, a well-managed investment portfolio can provide the necessary funds to support your endeavors. Investing gives you the ability to shape your financial future and have control over your financial destiny.

Investing is a powerful tool for securing long-term financial security and achieving your financial goals. It provides opportunities for wealth accumulation, retirement planning, risk management, and capitalizing on market opportunities. By investing wisely and staying committed to a long-term perspective, you can navigate the dynamic financial landscape, beat inflation, and build a solid financial foundation. Remember, investing involves risks, and it's important to conduct thorough research, seek professional advice when needed, and stay disciplined in your investment strategy. Start investing early, be patient, and let the power of compounding work in your favor to secure your long-term financial well-being.

CHAPTER TWO

Understanding the Investment Landscape

Overview of Different Asset Classes: Understanding Stocks, Bonds, Real Estate, and More

When it comes to investing, understanding the various asset classes is essential for building a diversified portfolio that aligns with your financial goals and risk tolerance. Each asset class offers unique characteristics and potential returns. Here is a brief overview of the most common asset classes—stocks, bonds, real estate, and more—helping you make informed investment decisions.

Stocks:

Stocks, also known as equities, represent ownership shares in publicly traded companies. When you purchase stocks, you become a partial owner and have the opportunity to benefit from the company's growth and profitability. Stocks offer the potential for capital appreciation and dividend income. However, they can also be volatile and subject to market fluctuations. Investing in individual stocks requires careful research and analysis, but for beginners or those seeking diversification, stock mutual funds or exchange-traded funds (ETFs) provide exposure to a diversified portfolio of stocks. ETFs are one of my favorite ways to invest. Even as an experienced investor, I still own many ETFs in my portfolio.

Bonds:

Bonds are debt instruments issued by governments, municipalities, and corporations. When you invest in bonds, you lend money to the issuer in exchange for periodic interest payments and the return of the principal amount upon maturity. Bonds are considered less risky than stocks and provide a fixed income stream. However, the returns on bonds are generally lower than those of stocks. Bonds can be classified into categories such as government bonds, corporate bonds, municipal bonds, and treasury bonds, each carrying its own risk and return profile. PIMCO bond funds are a great way to get started if this is an area you would like to invest in.

Real Estate:

Real estate encompasses residential, commercial, and industrial properties. Investing in real estate can be done through direct ownership of properties or indirectly through real estate investment trusts (REITs) or real estate mutual funds. Real estate offers the potential for capital appreciation and regular income through rental payments. It is considered a tangible asset and can provide diversification to a portfolio. However, real estate investments require careful evaluation of property location, market conditions, and property management considerations.

Commodities:

Commodities include physical goods such as gold, silver, oil, natural gas, agricultural products, and more. Investing in commodities can provide diversification and act as a hedge against inflation. Commodity prices are influenced by supply and demand dynamics and global economic factors. Investing in commodities can be done through commodity futures contracts, exchange-traded funds (ETFs), or specialized commodity-focused mutual funds.

Cash and Cash Equivalents:

Cash and cash equivalents refer to highly liquid assets, including bank deposits, money market funds, and short-term Treasury bills. These assets provide stability and immediate access to funds. While cash and cash equivalents may provide minimal returns, they play a crucial role in emergency funds and short-term financial needs. Maintaining an appropriate cash reserve is important for financial security and liquidity. I like to keep about 15-20% of my portfolio in cash so I can pounce on any opportunities as they arise.

Alternative Investments:

Alternative investments include hedge funds, private equity, venture capital, and derivatives. These investments are less traditional and often require sophisticated knowledge and expertise. Alternative investments aim to generate returns that are not correlated with traditional asset classes, providing potential diversification benefits. Due diligence and understanding the risks associated with alternative investments are crucial before allocating funds to these asset classes.

Understanding the various asset classes is essential for constructing a well-balanced investment portfolio. Stocks offer potential growth and ownership in companies, while bonds provide fixed income and relative stability. Real estate investments offer tangible assets and income potential. Commodities can serve as a hedge against inflation and provide diversification. Cash and cash equivalents provide liquidity and immediate access to funds. Alternative investments offer unique opportunities but require careful evaluation. By diversifying across different asset classes based on your investment goals and risk tolerance, you can achieve a well-rounded portfolio that balances potential returns with risk management. Remember, it's important to conduct thorough research and seek guidance from a professional.

Exploring Investment Vehicles: Mutual Funds, ETFs, Index Funds, and More

Investment vehicles are essential tools for individual investors to access a diverse range of assets and participate in financial markets. Among the popular investment vehicles are mutual funds, exchange-traded funds (ETFs), index funds, and others. Understanding the features, benefits, and differences of these vehicles can help investors make informed decisions and achieve their financial goals. In this section, we will explore the characteristics and advantages of various investment vehicles.

Mutual Funds:

Mutual funds pool money from multiple investors to invest in a diversified portfolio of stocks, bonds, or other securities. They are managed by professional fund managers who make investment decisions on behalf of the investors. Mutual funds offer diversification, as they invest in a wide range of securities. They also provide liquidity, allowing investors to buy or sell shares at the end of the trading day at the net asset value (NAV). Mutual funds are suitable for investors seeking professional management, diversification, and ease of investing.

Exchange-Traded Funds (ETFs):

ETFs are investment funds that trade on stock exchanges like individual stocks. They are similar to mutual funds in that they offer diversified portfolios of securities. However, unlike mutual funds, ETFs can be bought and sold throughout the trading day at market prices. ETFs can track various indexes, sectors, or asset classes, providing investors with exposure to specific market segments. They offer flexibility, liquidity, and lower expense ratios compared to some mutual funds.

Index Funds:

Index funds are a type of mutual fund or ETF that aim to replicate the performance of a specific market index, such as the S&P 500 or the Nasdaq-100. Rather than actively selecting securities, index funds passively hold the same securities as the index they track. This approach typically results in lower management fees and lower portfolio turnover. Index funds are suitable for investors seeking broad market exposure, long-term investing, and cost-effectiveness.

Individual Stocks and Bonds:

Investing in individual stocks and bonds involves buying shares of specific companies or purchasing bonds issued by governments, municipalities, or corporations. This approach requires investors to conduct research, analyze financial statements, and make individual investment decisions. Investing in individual stocks and bonds offers the potential for high returns but also carries higher risks. This strategy is suitable for investors who are comfortable with active management and have the time and expertise to analyze and monitor individual securities.

Real Estate Investment Trusts (REITs):

REITs are investment vehicles that pool funds from multiple investors to invest in real estate properties or mortgages. REITs can provide exposure to various types of real estate, including residential, commercial, or industrial properties. They offer liquidity and the potential for income through rental payments or interest payments. REITs are suitable for investors seeking real estate exposure without the need for direct property ownership.

Target-Date Funds:

Target-date funds are mutual funds or ETFs designed for retirement planning. They provide a diversified portfolio that automatically adjusts the asset allocation based on the investor's target retirement date. These funds gradually shift to a more conservative asset mix as the target date approaches, reducing risk. Target-date funds offer simplicity and convenience, making them suitable for investors looking for a hands-off approach to retirement planning.

Investment vehicles provide individual investors with access to a wide range of assets and investment strategies. Mutual funds, ETFs, index funds, individual stocks and bonds, REITs, and target-date funds all offer distinct advantages and cater to different investment objectives and risk tolerances. It is important for investors to assess their financial goals, risk appetite, and investment knowledge to choose the most suitable investment vehicles. Diversification, cost-effectiveness, liquidity, and professional management are among the key factors to consider when selecting an investment vehicle. Remember to conduct thorough research, review prospectuses, and consult with financial professionals before making investment decisions to ensure alignment with your financial objectives.

Understanding Risk and Return Trade-Offs in Investing

Investing involves a fundamental principle: the relationship between risk and return. In the world of finance, risk refers to the uncertainty or potential for loss, while return represents the gains or profits an investment can generate. Every investment decision requires a careful assessment of the risk and return trade-offs. Let's explore the concept of risk and return trade-offs in investing and how understanding this relationship is crucial for making informed investment decisions.

Risk and Return: A Basic Relationship:

Risk and return are inherently linked: the potential for higher returns is often accompanied by higher levels of risk. Investments that offer higher returns tend to carry more uncertainty and volatility. Conversely, investments with lower risk levels often yield lower potential returns. It is crucial to find a balance between risk and return that aligns with your investment goals, time horizon, and risk tolerance.

Asset Class Risk Profiles:

Different asset classes carry varying levels of risk. Stocks, for example, tend to be more volatile compared to bonds or cash equivalents. Real estate investments may be subject to market fluctuations and economic conditions. Understanding the risk profiles of different asset classes is essential when constructing a diversified investment portfolio. By spreading investments across various asset classes, investors can manage risk while aiming for an optimal level of return.

Systematic and Unsystematic Risk:

In investing, two types of risk are often discussed: systematic risk and unsystematic risk. Systematic risk, also known as market risk, is inherent in the overall market and affects all investments to some extent. Factors such as economic conditions, interest rates, and geopolitical events influence systematic risk. Unsystematic risk, on the other hand, is specific to individual investments or sectors. It can be mitigated through diversification. By diversifying investments across different asset classes, industries, and geographies, investors can reduce unsystematic risk while still benefiting from potential returns.

Risk Tolerance and Investment Horizon:

Investors have different risk tolerances, which refers to their ability and willingness to withstand potential losses. Risk tolerance is influenced by factors such as investment knowledge, financial goals, time horizon, and personal circumstances. Investors with a higher risk tolerance may be willing to accept greater volatility and invest in higher-risk assets, potentially seeking higher returns. Conversely, risk-averse investors may prioritize capital preservation and opt for more conservative investments. Additionally, the investment horizon—the length of time an investor plans to hold an investment—impacts the risk and return trade-offs. Longer investment horizons can allow investors to ride out short-term market fluctuations and potentially benefit from higher long-term returns.

Balancing Risk and Return:

Finding the right balance between risk and return is a crucial aspect of investment decision-making. Generally, higher-risk investments, such as stocks or emerging markets, have the potential for higher returns over the long term. Lower-risk investments, such as government bonds or cash equivalents, offer more stability but lower potential returns. It is important to assess your financial goals, investment knowledge, and risk tolerance to determine the appropriate mix of investments. Diversification across asset classes and regular portfolio reviews can help balance risk and return and optimize long-term investment performance.

Regular Monitoring and Risk Management:

Investing is an ongoing process that requires regular monitoring and risk management. Economic conditions, market trends, and individual investments can change over time. Monitoring your portfolio and making necessary adjustments can help align risk and return with your evolving investment goals. Additionally, risk management strategies, such as setting stop-loss orders, implementing trailing stops, or employing hedging techniques, can mitigate potential losses and protect against market downturns.

Understanding the relationship between risk and return is vital for successful investing. Investors must assess their risk tolerance, investment horizon, and financial goals to strike an appropriate balance between risk and return. Diversification, regular portfolio monitoring, and risk management strategies play crucial roles in optimizing investment outcomes. By aligning risk and return trade-offs with individual circumstances, investors can make informed decisions and pursue their financial objectives while managing the uncertainties of the financial markets. Remember, seeking professional advice and conducting thorough research are essential components of successful investing.

Economic Factors and Market Cycles: Understanding the Dynamics

The financial markets are influenced by a complex interplay of economic factors and market cycles. Economic conditions, such as inflation, interest rates, GDP growth, and employment levels, significantly impact market performance. Understanding these factors and their relationship to market cycles is crucial for investors seeking to navigate the ever-changing landscape of the financial world. In this section, we will explore the key economic factors and market cycles and how they shape investment opportunities and risks.

Economic Factors:

a. Inflation: Inflation refers to the general rise in prices over time. High inflation erodes purchasing power and can negatively impact investments. Conversely, moderate inflation can be beneficial for businesses and asset prices. Investors should monitor inflation indicators, such as Consumer Price Index (CPI) or Producer Price Index (PPI), as it affects interest rates and the value of investments.

b. Interest Rates: Interest rates influence borrowing costs, corporate profitability, and investor behavior. When interest rates are low, borrowing becomes cheaper, stimulating economic growth and potentially boosting stock prices. Conversely, rising interest rates can dampen economic activity and lead to market volatility. Monitoring central bank policies and indicators like the Federal Reserve's federal funds rate is essential for understanding interest rate trends.

c. GDP Growth: Gross Domestic Product (GDP) growth measures the overall economic output of a country. Strong GDP growth is often associated with increased corporate earnings and market expansion. Investors look for countries or regions with robust GDP growth as they offer potential investment opportunities. Monitoring GDP reports and economic indicators, such as industrial production or retail sales, can provide insights into economic health.

d. Employment Levels: Unemployment rates and job growth have a significant impact on consumer spending and overall economic stability. Low unemployment rates suggest a healthy labor market, higher consumer confidence, and potential economic growth. On the other hand, rising unemployment can lead to reduced consumer spending and slower economic activity. Investors monitor employment reports and indicators like non-farm payrolls to gauge the health of the labor market.

Market Cycles:

a. Bull Markets: Bull markets are characterized by rising stock prices and overall market optimism. They are often fueled by strong economic growth, low interest rates, and positive investor sentiment. Bull markets present opportunities for capital appreciation, but investors should exercise caution as valuations may become overextended.

b. Bear Markets: Bear markets occur when stock prices decline by 20% or more from their recent highs. They are typically driven by economic downturns, recessionary conditions, or significant market corrections. Bear markets can present buying opportunities for long-term investors seeking undervalued assets. Understanding the indicators of a bear market, such as prolonged market declines and negative economic indicators, is crucial for managing investment risks.

c. Market Volatility: Market volatility refers to rapid price fluctuations and uncertainty in the financial markets. It can be influenced by economic factors, geopolitical events, or investor sentiment. Volatile markets can create both opportunities and risks for investors. Risk management strategies, diversification, and a long-term perspective can help navigate market volatility effectively.

d. Market Sentiment: Market sentiment refers to the overall attitude and perception of investors towards the market. Positive sentiment can drive stock prices higher, while negative sentiment can lead to market selloffs. Sentiment indicators, such as surveys, investor confidence indices, and media coverage, provide insights into market expectations and can help investors gauge the prevailing sentiment.

Economic factors and market cycles play vital roles in shaping investment opportunities and risks. Understanding the relationship between economic indicators and market dynamics allows investors to make informed decisions. Monitoring key economic factors, such as inflation, interest rates, GDP growth, and employment levels, provides insights into overall economic health. Recognizing market cycles, from bull markets to bear markets and periods of volatility, helps investors adjust their strategies and manage risk. Remember, maintaining a diversified portfolio, conducting thorough research, and seeking professional advice are essential elements of successful investing in different economic environments.

CHAPTER THREE

Setting Financial Goals: Identifying Short-Term and Long-Term Objectives

Having clear financial objectives is essential for effective financial planning and achieving long-term financial success. Financial goals provide direction, motivation, and a framework for making sound financial decisions. However, it's important to distinguish between short-term and long-term objectives as they require different approaches and considerations. Let's explore the process of identifying short-term and long-term financial objectives and how they contribute to a comprehensive financial plan.

Short-Term Financial Objectives:

Short-term financial objectives typically encompass goals that can be achieved within a relatively brief time frame, usually within a year or less. These objectives often focus on immediate financial needs, lifestyle choices, and the building of a solid financial foundation. Some common short-term goals include:

a. Emergency Fund: Establishing an emergency fund to cover unforeseen expenses, such as medical emergencies or job loss. Aim to save three to six months' worth of living expenses in a liquid and easily accessible account.

b. Debt Repayment: Paying off high-interest debts, such as credit card balances or personal loans, to reduce financial burdens and improve cash flow.

c. Budgeting and Saving: Creating a budget to track expenses, reduce unnecessary spending, and allocate funds toward savings goals.

d. Education or Training: Investing in short-term educational programs or training to enhance skills, boost career prospects, or improve earning potential.

e. Small Purchases or Experiences: Setting aside funds for smaller purchases or experiences, such as a vacation, home renovation, or purchasing a new gadget from Amazon.

Long-Term Financial Objectives:

Long-term financial objectives involve goals that typically span several years or even decades. These objectives often require consistent planning, discipline, and a long-term perspective. Long-term goals focus on wealth accumulation, retirement planning, and achieving significant milestones. Some common long-term goals include:

a. Retirement Planning: Building a retirement nest egg by regularly contributing to retirement accounts, such as a 401(k), IRA, or pension plan, to ensure financial security in later years.

b. Wealth Accumulation: Investing in diverse asset classes, such as stocks, bonds, real estate, or mutual funds, with the goal of growing wealth over an extended period.

c. Education Funding: Saving for children's education expenses, such as college tuition, by utilizing tax-advantaged accounts like 529 plans or education savings accounts.

d. Homeownership: Saving for a down payment and purchasing a home to build equity and establish a stable living situation.

e. Estate Planning: Creating an estate plan to protect assets, ensure the smooth transfer of wealth to beneficiaries, and minimize estate taxes.

Considerations for Goal Identification:

a. Time Horizon: Differentiate between short-term and long-term goals based on the desired timeframe for achieving each objective. Short-term goals require immediate action, while long-term goals require sustained efforts over an extended period.

b. Specificity and Measurability: Define financial goals in specific and measurable terms. For example, instead of setting a vague goal like "save more money," specify an amount to save each month or year.

c. Prioritization: Assess the importance and urgency of each goal to establish a hierarchy and allocate resources accordingly.

Prioritizing goals helps avoid spreading resources too thin and ensures focus on the most critical objectives.

d. Flexibility: Recognize that financial goals may evolve over time due to changing circumstances, new opportunities, or revised priorities. Periodically review and adjust your objectives as necessary.

Identifying short-term and long-term financial objectives is a fundamental step in effective financial planning. Short-term goals address immediate financial needs and establish a solid foundation, while long-term goals focus on wealth accumulation, retirement planning, and major milestones. By setting clear objectives, you can develop a comprehensive financial plan, allocate resources wisely, and stay motivated on your journey toward financial success. Remember, regular monitoring, reassessment, and adjustments are essential to align your goals with changing circumstances and ensure continued progress.

Inflation and Taxes: Their Impact on Investment Returns

Investors must consider various factors that can impact investment returns. Two critical factors are inflation and taxes. Inflation erodes the purchasing power of money over time, while taxes can reduce the overall returns on investments. Understanding the impact of inflation and taxes is crucial for investors to make informed decisions and effectively preserve and grow their wealth. In this chapter, we will delve into how inflation and taxes affect investment returns and explore strategies to mitigate their impact.

The Impact of Inflation on Investment Returns:

a. Understanding Inflation: Inflation refers to the general rise in prices over time. It erodes the value of money, reducing the purchasing power of future cash flows. Inflation can have a significant impact on investment returns, especially over the long term.

b. Effects on Fixed-Income Investments: Fixed-income investments, such as bonds or certificates of deposit (CDs), are particularly vulnerable to inflation. As inflation rises, the fixed interest payments from these investments may not keep pace with increasing prices, resulting in a decrease in real purchasing power.

c. Effects on Stocks and Equities: While stocks historically offer a potential hedge against inflation, not all companies can maintain profitability during periods of high inflation. Investors should consider investing in sectors that can adapt to inflationary pressures and generate real growth in revenues and earnings.

d. Strategies to Mitigate Inflationary Impact: Investors can employ several strategies to mitigate the impact of inflation on investment returns. These include investing in inflation-protected securities like Treasury Inflation-Protected Securities (TIPS), diversifying across asset classes, and considering investments in companies with pricing power or commodities that tend to perform well during inflationary periods.

The Impact of Taxes on Investment Returns:

a. Understanding Taxes on Investment Returns: Taxes can significantly impact investment returns by reducing the amount of income or gains retained by the investor. The tax implications vary depending on the type of investment and the holding period.

b. Types of Investment Taxes: Common investment taxes include capital gains taxes, dividend taxes, and interest income taxes. The rates and rules for these taxes differ between countries and can also depend on an individual's tax bracket and the length of time an investment is held.

c. Tax-Efficient Investing Strategies: Investors can employ several strategies to minimize the impact of taxes on investment returns. These include utilizing tax-advantaged accounts like Individual Retirement Accounts (IRAs) or 401(k) plans, employing tax-loss harvesting techniques to offset capital gains with capital losses, and utilizing tax-efficient investment vehicles like index funds or exchange-traded funds (ETFs).

d. Long-Term Capital Gains: Investors may benefit from favorable tax rates on long-term capital gains, which are typically lower than short-term capital gains rates. Holding investments for more than one year may qualify for long-term capital gains treatment, reducing the overall tax liability.

Balancing Inflation and Taxes with Investment Objectives:

a. Considering Risk and Return: Investors must strike a balance between managing the impact of inflation and taxes while pursuing their investment objectives. It requires assessing risk tolerance, investment horizon, and the desired rate of return.

b. Diversification and Asset Allocation: Diversifying investments across different asset classes and sectors can help manage inflation risk and reduce tax burdens. Proper asset allocation aligns with an investor's risk profile and investment goals.

c. Regular Monitoring and Adjustments: The investment landscape, inflation rates, and tax regulations are subject to change. Regularly monitoring investments and adapting strategies based on evolving economic conditions and tax laws is essential to optimize returns and minimize risk.

Inflation and taxes are important considerations that can significantly impact investment returns. By understanding the effects of inflation on different asset classes and employing tax-efficient strategies, investors can preserve and enhance their wealth over time. Regular monitoring, periodic adjustments, and seeking professional advice are essential in navigating the complexities of inflation and taxes to achieve long-term investment success.

Estimating Retirement Needs and Planning for a Secure Future

Retirement planning is a crucial aspect of financial management. To ensure a comfortable and secure retirement, it's essential to estimate your retirement needs accurately and develop a comprehensive retirement plan. This chapter will guide you through the process of estimating your retirement needs and provide insights into effective retirement planning strategies.

Estimating Retirement Needs:

a. Assessing Current Expenses: Begin by evaluating your current expenses to establish a baseline for estimating your retirement needs. Consider your housing costs, daily living expenses, healthcare expenses, travel aspirations, and any other lifestyle factors that may impact your retirement budget.

b. Factoring Inflation: Account for inflation when estimating your retirement needs. Inflation erodes the purchasing power of money over time, so it's important to project your expenses based on future inflation rates. A common approach is to assume an average inflation rate of 2-3% per year.

c. Consideration of Healthcare Costs: Healthcare expenses tend to increase during retirement. Research and estimate potential healthcare costs, including insurance premiums, medication, and long-term care expenses. Consider the potential impact of Medicare and supplemental insurance on your retirement healthcare costs.

d. Lifestyle Considerations: Determine the type of lifestyle you envision for your retirement years. Will you downsize, travel extensively, or pursue expensive hobbies? Understanding your desired lifestyle will help you estimate the necessary funds to support it.

e. Life Expectancy: Consider your life expectancy when estimating retirement needs. Plan for a longer retirement to ensure you have adequate savings to sustain yourself throughout your golden years. Various online tools and calculators can assist in estimating life expectancy based on factors such as demographics, health, and lifestyle choices.

Retirement Planning Strategies:

a. Start Early: The earlier you start saving for retirement, the more time your investments have to grow. Take advantage of compounding returns by consistently contributing to retirement accounts, such as employer-sponsored plans like 401(k)s or individual retirement accounts (IRAs).

b. Determine Retirement Income Sources: Identify potential sources of retirement income, including Social Security benefits, pensions, and investment returns. Understand how these income sources factor into your overall retirement plan and consider the optimal time to start drawing from them.

c. Set Realistic Savings Goals: Establish specific savings goals based on your estimated retirement needs. Determine how much you need to save each year to reach those goals and adjust your budget and lifestyle accordingly. Automate contributions to retirement accounts to ensure consistent savings.

d. Tax-Efficient Retirement Savings: Maximize your retirement savings by taking advantage of tax-efficient investment vehicles like 401(k)s, IRAs, and Roth IRAs. Understand the tax implications of each account type and choose the ones that align with your tax situation and retirement goals.

e. Diversify Your Investments: Diversification is key to mitigating investment risk. Allocate your retirement savings across different asset classes, such as stocks, bonds, and real estate, to spread risk and potentially enhance returns. Consider consulting a financial advisor to determine the appropriate asset allocation based on your risk tolerance and time horizon.

f. Regularly Review and Adjust: Regularly review your retirement plan and make necessary adjustments. Factors like changing life circumstances, market conditions, and personal goals may require modifications to your savings and investment strategy. Stay informed about updates to retirement laws and regulations that may impact your plan.

Estimating retirement needs and planning for a secure future is crucial for a comfortable retirement. By accurately estimating your expenses, accounting for inflation, and considering healthcare costs and lifestyle aspirations, you can develop a realistic retirement plan. Implementing strategies like starting early, diversifying investments, and maximizing tax-efficient retirement accounts will set you on the path to a financially stable retirement. Regularly review and adjust your plan to ensure it remains aligned with your changing circumstances and retirement goals.

CHAPTER FOUR

Budgeting and Managing Expenses: Building a Strong Financial Foundation

Effective budgeting and expense management are fundamental skills for achieving financial stability and reaching your financial goals. By understanding your income, tracking expenses, and making conscious spending decisions, you can take control of your finances and make your money work for you. Now, let's walk through the process of budgeting and managing expenses, empowering you to build a solid financial foundation.

Creating a Budget:

a. Assessing Income: Begin by calculating your total income, including salary, wages, side hustles, investments, and any other sources of income. Understanding your income streams is crucial for effective budgeting.

b. Identifying Fixed and Variable Expenses: Differentiate between fixed expenses (e.g., rent, mortgage payments, insurance premiums) and variable expenses (e.g., groceries, entertainment, dining out). Fixed expenses tend to remain consistent, while variable expenses can fluctuate from month to month.

c. Tracking Expenses: Monitor your spending habits by tracking expenses diligently. Use budgeting apps, spreadsheets, or even pen and paper to record your expenses. Categorize your expenses to gain insights into your spending patterns.

d. Analyzing Spending Patterns: Regularly review your spending patterns to identify areas where you may be overspending or where you can make adjustments. Look for opportunities to reduce discretionary expenses and prioritize essential needs.

Budgeting Strategies:

a. 50/30/20 Rule: Allocate your after-tax income using the 50/30/20 rule. Dedicate 50% of your income to necessities (e.g., housing, utilities, transportation), 30% to discretionary spending (e.g., entertainment, dining out), and 20% to savings and debt repayment.

b. Zero-Based Budgeting: With zero-based budgeting, assign every dollar of your income to a specific purpose. Ensure that your total income minus total expenses equals zero by assigning funds to savings, investments, debt repayment, and financial goals.

c. Emergency Fund: Prioritize building an emergency fund to cover unexpected expenses and financial emergencies. Aim to save three to six months' worth of living expenses in a separate, easily accessible account.

d. Debt Management: Create a strategy to manage and reduce debt. Prioritize high-interest debts, such as credit card balances or personal loans, and consider debt consolidation or refinancing options to lower interest rates and simplify payments.

Expense Management Techniques:

a. Differentiating Wants vs. Needs: Distinguish between wants and needs to make conscious spending decisions. Prioritize essential needs over discretionary wants and consider alternatives or cost-saving measures for non-essential expenses.

b. Comparison Shopping: Before making significant purchases, research and compare prices, quality, and reviews. Take advantage of sales, discounts, or loyalty programs to get the best value for your money. And don't forget to clip coupons. Every penny you save advances you closer to your goal.

c. Negotiating and Renegotiating Bills: Contact service providers (e.g., cable, internet, insurance) to negotiate better rates or explore alternative options. Regularly review and renegotiate bills to ensure you're getting the most cost-effective services.

d. Automating Savings: Set up automatic transfers from your checking account to savings or investment accounts. Automating savings ensures consistent contributions and helps you stay on track with your financial goals.

Ongoing Expense Monitoring:

a. Regular Expense Reviews: Continuously monitor your expenses and budget to identify areas of improvement and make necessary adjustments. Regularly track your progress and celebrate milestones as you achieve your financial goals.

b. Financial Tools and Apps: Utilize budgeting apps, expense trackers, or personal finance software to simplify expense management and gain valuable insights into your financial habits.

c. Seeking Professional Advice: Consider consulting a financial advisor or planner for expert guidance on budgeting, expense management, and financial planning. They can provide personalized strategies and help you optimize your financial journey.

Budgeting and managing expenses are vital components of financial success. By creating a realistic budget, tracking expenses, and implementing effective expense management techniques, you can take control of your finances and achieve your financial goals. Regularly review and adjust your budget, seek opportunities to reduce expenses, and make conscious spending decisions to build a strong financial foundation.

Reducing and Managing Debt: Regain Financial Freedom

Debt can be a significant burden on your financial well-being, hindering your ability to achieve your goals and build wealth. However, by implementing effective debt reduction and management strategies, you can take control of your financial situation and pave the way to a debt-free future. This chapter will guide you through the process of reducing and managing debt, providing you with the tools and knowledge to regain financial freedom.

Assessing Your Debt Situation:

a. Identifying and Organizing Debt: Begin by compiling a comprehensive list of all your debts, including credit cards, loans, student loans, and mortgages. Note the outstanding balances, interest rates, minimum monthly payments, and due dates for each debt.

b. Understanding Interest Rates: Prioritize debts with higher interest rates as they can accumulate more interest over time. Assess whether any debts have variable interest rates and understand how potential interest rate changes may impact your repayments.

c. Evaluating Debt-to-Income Ratio: Calculate your debt-to-income ratio, which is the percentage of your monthly income that goes toward debt payments. This assessment helps you understand your debt load relative to your income and guides your repayment strategy.

Developing a Debt Repayment Plan:

a. Snowball Method: With the snowball method, focus on paying off the smallest debts first while making minimum payments on other debts. Once a smaller debt is paid off, roll the amount you were paying toward that debt into the next smallest debt. This approach provides a psychological boost as you see debts being eliminated.

b. Avalanche Method: The avalanche method prioritizes debts with the highest interest rates. Make minimum payments on all debts while allocating any extra funds toward the debt with the highest interest rate. Once that debt is paid off, move on to the debt with the next highest interest rate.

c. Debt Consolidation: Consider consolidating high-interest debts into a single loan or credit card with a lower interest rate. Debt consolidation simplifies repayment and may reduce overall interest costs. However, assess the terms and fees associated with consolidation options before proceeding.

d. Negotiating with Creditors: If you're struggling to meet your debt obligations, contact your creditors to discuss possible options. They may be willing to negotiate a repayment plan, lower interest rates, or waive late fees. Communicate your financial situation honestly and proactively seek solutions.

Managing Debt Responsibly:

a. Creating a Realistic Budget: Develop a budget that prioritizes debt repayment. Allocate a portion of your income toward paying down debt while ensuring you cover essential living expenses. Avoid accumulating additional debt by living within your means.

b. Controlling Credit Card Usage: Limit credit card spending and avoid carrying balances whenever possible. Paying off credit card balances in full each month helps you avoid high-interest charges and reduces the risk of accumulating more debt.

c. Building an Emergency Fund: Establish an emergency fund to cover unexpected expenses. Having readily available savings can prevent you from relying on credit cards or taking on more debt during financial emergencies.

d. Seeking Professional Guidance: If your debt situation is overwhelming or complex, consider seeking assistance from a credit counselor or financial advisor. They can provide personalized advice, negotiate with creditors on your behalf, and help you develop a sustainable debt management plan.

Staying Motivated and Persistent:

a. Celebrating Milestones: Acknowledge and celebrate each debt milestone you achieve. Whether it's paying off a credit card or reaching a specific debt reduction target, recognizing your progress reinforces your determination to continue on your debt-free journey.

b. Regularly Reviewing and Adjusting: Periodically reassess your debt repayment plan to ensure its effectiveness. Adjust your strategy as needed based on changes in income, interest rates, or financial goals. Stay proactive and adaptable in your approach.

c. Adopting Healthy Financial Habits: Embrace healthy financial habits that promote long-term debt management and financial well-being. These may include budgeting, saving, and making informed spending decisions to avoid falling back into debt.

Reducing and managing debt is a crucial step toward achieving financial freedom. By assessing your debt situation, developing a repayment plan, and adopting responsible financial habits, you can regain control over your finances. Stay motivated, seek professional guidance when needed, and remember that with persistence and discipline, you can overcome debt and pave the way for a brighter financial future.

Establishing an Emergency Fund: Building Financial Resilience

Life is full of unexpected events and financial emergencies can strike at any time. Establishing an emergency fund is a critical step in securing your financial well-being and protecting yourself from unforeseen circumstances. This chapter will guide you through the process of building and maintaining an emergency fund, helping you establish a solid financial safety net.

Understanding the Importance of an Emergency Fund:

a. Financial Security: An emergency fund provides a buffer against unexpected expenses, such as medical emergencies, job loss, home repairs, or car repairs. It safeguards your financial stability and reduces the need to rely on credit cards or loans during times of crisis.

b. Peace of Mind: Knowing that you have a dedicated fund to handle emergencies brings peace of mind and reduces stress. It allows you to face unexpected situations with confidence and without compromising your long-term financial goals.

Setting Goals for Your Emergency Fund:

a. Assessing Your Needs: Evaluate your personal circumstances and consider factors such as monthly expenses, dependents, job stability, and health conditions. Aim to save enough to cover at least three to six months' worth of essential living expenses.

b. Adjusting for Specific Situations: Depending on your situation, you may need to save more or less than the standard three to six months' worth of expenses. Factors such as job security, industry volatility, health concerns, and support networks should influence your savings target.

c. Considering Other Financial Goals: Balance the priority of building an emergency fund with other financial goals, such as paying off high-interest debt or saving for retirement. Find a balance that allows you to contribute to your emergency fund while still making progress towards other objectives.

Building Your Emergency Fund:

a. Determine a Realistic Timeline: Establish a timeline for building your emergency fund based on your savings capacity and financial goals. Set specific monthly or bi-monthly savings targets to stay on track.

b. Automating Contributions: Make saving for emergencies a priority by automating contributions to your emergency fund. Set up automatic transfers from your checking account to a separate savings account specifically designated for emergencies.

c. Treat It as a Monthly Expense: Consider your emergency fund contribution as a non-negotiable monthly expense, just like rent or utility bills. Make it a habit to set aside a portion of your income for your emergency fund before allocating funds to other discretionary expenses.

d. Windfalls and Extra Income: Utilize windfalls, such as tax refunds, bonuses, or unexpected cash inflows, to boost your emergency fund. Direct any extra income towards your savings to accelerate the growth of your fund.

Managing and Maintaining Your Emergency Fund:

a. Separate and Accessible Account: Keep your emergency fund separate from your regular checking or savings accounts to avoid temptation or accidental spending. Choose an account that offers easy access, such as a high-yield savings account or a money market account.

b. Regular Evaluation and Adjustments: Periodically review your emergency fund savings to ensure it aligns with your current financial situation and needs. Adjust the target amount if circumstances change, such as an increase in expenses or a shift in income.

c. Replenishing After an Emergency: If you need to tap into your emergency fund, prioritize replenishing the withdrawn amount as soon as possible. Resume your regular contributions to rebuild the fund to its recommended level.

d. Keep it for Emergencies Only: Resist the temptation to dip into your emergency fund for non-essential expenses or discretionary purchases. Maintain the discipline to use the fund solely for genuine emergencies.

Expanding the Safety Net:

a. Insurance Coverage: Review your insurance policies, including health, home, auto, and disability insurance, to ensure you have adequate coverage. Insurance can provide additional protection against unexpected events and reduce the need to rely solely on your emergency fund.

b. Long-Term Planning: As you strengthen your emergency fund, consider expanding your financial safety net with long-term planning strategies. This may include building retirement savings, investing in diversified portfolios, or exploring other income-generating opportunities.

Establishing an emergency fund is a cornerstone of financial stability. By setting goals, consistently contributing, and maintaining your emergency fund, you can safeguard your financial well-being and face unexpected events with confidence. Make building an emergency fund a priority, stay committed to your savings goals, and enjoy the peace of mind that comes from knowing you're prepared for whatever challenges may arise.

The Importance of Insurance Coverage: Protecting Your Financial Well-Being

Insurance serves as a crucial component of a comprehensive financial plan, providing protection against unforeseen events that could otherwise jeopardize your financial stability. In this chapter, we will explore the importance of insurance coverage and the various types of insurance policies available to help safeguard your assets, health, and future.

Understanding the Role of Insurance:

a. Risk Management: Insurance acts as a risk management tool, transferring potential financial losses from an individual or entity to an insurance provider. It helps mitigate the financial impact of unexpected events, ensuring you are not solely responsible for covering the costs.

b. Financial Protection: Insurance provides a safety net, shielding your assets, income, and loved ones from significant financial losses due to accidents, illnesses, natural disasters, or legal liabilities.

c. Peace of Mind: Knowing you have adequate insurance coverage brings peace of mind, allowing you to focus on other aspects of your life without constant worry about the financial consequences of unexpected events.

Types of Insurance Coverage:

a. Health Insurance: Health insurance covers medical expenses, including doctor visits, hospital stays, prescription medications, and preventive care. It helps protect against high healthcare costs and ensures access to quality healthcare services.

b. Life Insurance: Life insurance provides financial support to your beneficiaries in the event of your death. It can help replace lost income, cover funeral expenses, pay off debts, and ensure the financial well-being of your loved ones.

c. Disability Insurance: Disability insurance offers income replacement if you become unable to work due to a disability or illness. It safeguards your financial stability and ensures you can meet your financial obligations even if you are unable to work.

d. Property Insurance: Property insurance protects your physical assets, such as your home, vehicle, or personal belongings, against damage, theft, or loss. It provides financial compensation to repair or replace damaged property.

e. Liability Insurance: Liability insurance covers legal liabilities arising from accidents or injuries that occur on your property or as a result of your actions. It helps protect your assets and provides financial support in legal disputes.

f. Long-Term Care Insurance: Long-term care insurance covers the costs associated with extended healthcare services, such as nursing home care, assisted living, or in-home care. It helps protect your savings and assets from being depleted by long-term care expenses.

Assessing Your Insurance Needs:

a. Evaluate Risks and Vulnerabilities: Assess your personal circumstances, taking into account factors such as your age, health, dependents, assets, and liabilities. Identify potential risks and vulnerabilities that could significantly impact your financial well-being.

b. Consider Legal Requirements: Some types of insurance, such as auto insurance or workers' compensation, may be legally required in certain jurisdictions. Ensure you comply with any mandatory insurance regulations.

c. Analyze Personal Goals and Priorities: Align your insurance coverage with your financial goals and priorities. Consider factors such as the financial needs of your dependents, desired level of protection, and comfort with risk.

Selecting Adequate Coverage:

a. Work with an Insurance Professional: Consult an experienced insurance agent or broker who can provide guidance and help you navigate the complexities of insurance policies. They can assess your needs, recommend suitable coverage options, and help you find competitive premiums.

b. Review Policy Terms and Coverage: Thoroughly review insurance policies, including the terms, coverage limits, deductibles, and exclusions. Understand what events or circumstances are covered and ensure the policy adequately meets your needs.

c. Avoid Underinsuring or Over insuring: Strive for a balance between underinsurance (insufficient coverage) and over insurance (unnecessarily high coverage). Adequately protect yourself without paying for unnecessary coverage that exceeds your needs.

d. Regularly Review and Update: Revisit your insurance coverage periodically to ensure it remains aligned with your evolving needs and circumstances. Major life events, such as marriage, parenthood, or purchasing a home, may require adjustments to your insurance policies.

Insurance coverage is vital to your overall financial plan, protecting against unexpected events and potential financial hardships. By understanding the role of insurance, assessing your needs, and selecting adequate coverage, you can safeguard your assets, income, and loved ones. Prioritize insurance as part of your financial strategy and enjoy the peace of mind that comes from knowing you have taken steps to protect your financial well-being.

CHAPTER FIVE

Determining Your Risk Tolerance and Investment Time Horizon: Keys to Successful Investing

Successful investing requires aligning your investment strategy with your risk tolerance and investment time horizon. These two factors play a crucial role in shaping your investment decisions, asset allocation, and overall portfolio management. This section will explore how to determine your risk tolerance and investment time horizon, helping you make informed investment choices that align with your financial goals and comfort level.

Understanding Risk Tolerance:

Risk tolerance refers to your willingness and ability to endure potential losses in pursuit of investment returns. It is influenced by several factors, including your financial situation, investment goals, investment knowledge, and personal attitudes toward risk.

Assessing Your Financial Situation:

Consider your current financial position, including your income, expenses, assets, liabilities, and emergency fund. A stable financial foundation provides greater flexibility to take on moderate to higher investment risks.

Identifying Investment Goals:

Define your investment objectives, such as saving for retirement, purchasing a home, funding education, or achieving long-term growth. Goals that have longer time horizons may allow for a higher risk tolerance as there is more time to ride out market fluctuations.

Evaluating Investment Knowledge and Experience:

Be honest about your understanding of investing concepts, market dynamics, and investment products. Investors with higher knowledge and experience may be more comfortable taking on greater investment risks.

Assessing Emotional Resilience:

Consider your emotional response to market volatility and potential investment losses. Some investors may feel uneasy or anxious during market downturns, while others may remain calm and focused on long-term goals.

Determining Investment Time Horizon:

Investment time horizon refers to the duration you plan to remain invested in a particular investment or portfolio. It can range from short-term (less than one year) to long-term (10 years or more).

Define Your Time Horizon:

Identify the specific time frame within which you expect to achieve your investment goals. For example, retirement planning may have a time horizon of 20 to 30 years, while saving for a down payment on a house may have a time horizon of 3 to 5 years.

Consider Flexibility:

Evaluate whether your investment goals have flexibility in terms of timing. Some goals, such as education expenses, may have a fixed time frame, while others, like general wealth accumulation, may allow for more flexibility.

Evaluate Risk Capacity:

Your time horizon influences your risk capacity, which is the ability to recover from short-term market fluctuations. Longer time horizons generally allow for a higher risk tolerance, as there is more opportunity to ride out market downturns and potentially benefit from long-term market growth.

Regularly Review and Adjust:

As you approach your investment goals, regularly review and adjust your investment time horizon. Shorter time horizons may necessitate a shift toward more conservative investments to preserve capital, while longer time horizons may allow for a more growth-oriented strategy.

Finding the Right Balance:

Finding the right balance between risk tolerance and investment time horizon is crucial for building a well-suited investment portfolio.

Consult with a Financial Advisor:

Consider seeking guidance from a financial advisor who can assess your risk tolerance, investment goals, and time horizon. They can provide professional expertise and help design an investment strategy tailored to your needs.

Diversify Your Portfolio:

Diversification is a key risk management strategy that involves spreading your investments across different asset classes, sectors, and geographical regions. It can help mitigate the impact of market volatility and reduce risk.

Regularly Monitor and Rebalance:

Regularly review your investment portfolio to ensure it remains aligned with your risk tolerance and time horizon. Market fluctuations and changes in personal circumstances may warrant adjustments to maintain the desired risk-return profile.

Determining your risk tolerance and investment time horizon is essential for successful investing. By understanding your financial situation, investment goals, emotional resilience, and time frame, you can make informed investment decisions and construct a portfolio that aligns with your unique circumstances. Remember that risk tolerance and time horizon are not fixed but can evolve over time, so regularly reassess, and adjust your investment strategy as needed.

Creating an Investment Strategy and Asset Allocation: Building a Path to Financial Success

Creating a robust investment strategy and determining the appropriate asset allocation are key components of successful investing. These decisions lay the foundation for your portfolio's risk-return profile and long-term growth potential. Let's now explore the steps involved in creating an investment strategy and establishing an asset allocation that aligns with your financial goals, risk tolerance, and time horizon.

Defining Your Investment Objectives:

a. Identify Financial Goals: Determine your short-term and long-term financial objectives, such as retirement savings, education funding, or purchasing a home. Clearly defining your goals helps shape your investment strategy.

b. Quantify Risk Tolerance: Evaluate your risk tolerance by considering factors such as your financial situation, emotional resilience, and investment knowledge. This assessment will guide your asset allocation decisions.

Conducting Investment Research:

a. Understand Different Asset Classes: Familiarize yourself with various asset classes, including stocks, bonds, cash equivalents, real estate, and alternative investments. Learn about their risk and return characteristics to make informed decisions.

b. Analyze Historical Performance: Study the historical performance of different asset classes and their correlations. This analysis will help you understand how different investments behave in different market conditions.

c. Consider Market Outlook: Stay informed about current market trends, economic indicators, and geopolitical factors that can impact investment returns. This information will guide your asset allocation decisions and portfolio rebalancing.

Determining Asset Allocation:

a. Risk-Return Trade-off: Assess your risk tolerance and desired level of return. Generally, higher-risk investments have the potential for higher returns but also greater volatility. Determine the optimal balance between risk and return that aligns with your objectives.

b. Diversification: Build a diversified portfolio by allocating your investments across different asset classes, sectors, and regions. Diversification helps reduce portfolio risk by spreading exposure and potentially capturing gains from multiple sources.

c. Age and Time Horizon Considerations: Adjust your asset allocation based on your age and investment time horizon. Younger investors with longer time horizons can typically tolerate more risk and allocate a larger portion to growth-oriented investments.

Implementing Your Investment Strategy:

a. Selecting Investments: Choose specific investments within each asset class that align with your investment strategy. Consider factors such as historical performance, fund management, expenses, and risk factors.

b. Dollar-Cost Averaging: Consider implementing a dollar-cost averaging strategy, where you invest a fixed amount regularly regardless of market conditions. This approach helps smooth out market fluctuations and potentially lower the average cost of investments.

c. Rebalancing: Regularly review and rebalance your portfolio to maintain your desired asset allocation. Market movements may cause your portfolio to drift from the intended allocation, so periodically adjust your holdings to realign with your targets.

Monitoring and Reviewing Your Portfolio:

a. Regular Performance Evaluation: Monitor the performance of your investments relative to your benchmarks and objectives. Assess if adjustments are needed to optimize your portfolio's risk-return profile.

b. Life Changes and Adjustments: Reassess your investment strategy when significant life changes occur, such as career shifts, marriage, or the birth of children. Adjustments may be necessary to reflect new financial goals or risk tolerance levels.

c. Seek Professional Advice: Consider consulting a financial advisor for guidance on investment strategy, asset allocation, and portfolio management. An advisor can provide expertise and help tailor your investment approach to your unique circumstances.

Creating an investment strategy and determining asset allocation are crucial steps in building a successful investment portfolio. By defining your goals, conducting thorough research, determining asset allocation, implementing your strategy, and monitoring your portfolio, you can increase your chances of achieving your financial objectives. Regularly review and adjust your investment strategy as needed to adapt to changing market conditions and personal circumstances. Remember, a well-constructed investment strategy is a roadmap to financial success.

Selecting a Brokerage Account and Understanding Investment Costs: Navigating the Path to Efficient Investing

Selecting the right brokerage account and understanding investment costs are crucial steps in building a successful investment portfolio. These decisions impact the accessibility of investment options, transaction fees, and ongoing expenses. In this chapter, we will explore the factors to consider when choosing a brokerage account and delve into the various investment costs you may encounter along your investment journey.

Assessing Your Needs and Goals:

a. Determine Your Investment Objectives: Clarify your investment goals, risk tolerance, and time horizon. This assessment will help you choose a brokerage account that aligns with your specific needs.

b. Consider Your Trading Frequency: Determine how frequently you plan to trade investments. If you are an active trader, you may prioritize a brokerage account with low trading commissions and advanced trading tools.

c. Evaluate Your Asset Class Preferences: Consider the types of investments you intend to hold. Different brokerage accounts may offer varying access to stocks, bonds, mutual funds, exchange-traded funds (ETFs), options, or other investment vehicles.

Comparing Brokerage Account Features:

a. Trading Commissions and Fees: Compare the costs associated with trading, such as commissions per trade, account maintenance fees, and inactivity fees. Be mindful of any fee structures that could significantly impact your investment returns.

b. Investment Options: Evaluate the range of investment options available through the brokerage account. Ensure that the account provides access to the asset classes and investment products you desire.

c. Research and Educational Resources: Assess the quality and availability of research tools, educational materials, and market analysis provided by the brokerage. These resources can be valuable for making informed investment decisions.

d. Customer Service and Support: Consider the level of customer service and support provided by the brokerage. Prompt and reliable assistance can be essential when troubleshooting account issues or seeking investment advice.

Understanding Investment Costs:

a. Expense Ratios: When investing in mutual funds or ETFs, pay attention to expense ratios. These ratios represent the annual fees charged by the fund or ETF provider and can impact your investment returns over time.

b. Trading Fees and Commissions: Be aware of the fees associated with buying or selling investments, including commissions, transaction fees, and bid-ask spreads. These costs can impact the overall performance of your portfolio, especially for frequent traders.

c. Account Management Fees: Some brokerages may charge annual or quarterly account management fees, especially for managed accounts or certain account types. Understand these fees and compare them across different brokerage options.

d. Margin Interest and Borrowing Costs: If you plan to utilize margin trading or borrow against your investments, be aware of the interest rates and costs associated with these services. High borrowing costs can erode your investment returns.

Conducting Due Diligence:

a. Read Brokerage Reviews and Ratings: Research and read independent reviews of brokerage firms to gauge their reputation, reliability, and customer satisfaction. Consider factors such as the platform's stability, ease of use, and security measures.

b. Investigate Account Protection: Understand the level of account protection provided by the brokerage. Look for brokerages that are members of regulatory bodies or offer additional insurance coverage to protect your investments.

c. Consider Integration with Other Financial Services: If you have other financial accounts, such as bank accounts or retirement accounts, consider a brokerage that offers seamless integration and consolidates your financial information.

Selecting a brokerage account and understanding investment

costs are critical steps in building an efficient and cost-effective investment portfolio. Carefully assess your needs and goals, compare brokerage account features, and consider the various investment costs associated with trading and maintaining your portfolio. By making informed decisions, you can find a brokerage account that meets your requirements and maximize your investment returns. Regularly review your brokerage account and costs to ensure they align with your evolving needs and goals.

Harnessing the Power of Dollar-Cost Averaging and Compounding: Building Wealth through Consistency

Dollar-cost averaging, and the power of compounding are two fundamental concepts that can significantly enhance your long-term investment results. By understanding and utilizing these strategies effectively, you can build wealth, mitigate market volatility, and maximize the growth potential of your investments. Let's discuss the principles of dollar-cost averaging and the power of compounding, illustrating how they work in tandem to accelerate your path to financial success.

Dollar-Cost Averaging: Smoothing Out Market Volatility

a. What is Dollar-Cost Averaging? Dollar-cost averaging is an investment strategy that involves consistently investing a fixed amount of money at regular intervals, regardless of market conditions. It enables you to purchase more shares when prices are low and fewer shares when prices are high, effectively smoothing out the impact of market volatility.

b. Benefits of Dollar-Cost Averaging:

i. Eliminates the Need to Time the Market: Dollar-cost averaging removes the pressure of trying to time the market, as investments are made consistently over time.

ii. Mitigates Emotional Decision-Making: By sticking to a disciplined investment plan, you are less likely to be swayed by short-term market fluctuations or succumb to impulsive decisions.

iii. Potential for Lower Average Cost: Over time, purchasing more shares when prices are low can result in a lower average cost per share, maximizing your potential gains when the market rebounds.

c. Implementing Dollar-Cost Averaging:

i. Choose a Regular Investment Schedule: Set a fixed amount and determine the frequency at which you will invest, such as monthly or quarterly.

ii. Automate Your Investments: Set up automatic contributions from your bank account to your investment account to ensure consistency and discipline.

iii. Stay Committed to the Strategy: Regardless of market conditions, maintain your regular investment contributions and avoid trying to time the market.

The Power of Compounding: Accelerating Wealth Accumulation

a. Understanding Compound Interest: Compound interest is the process of earning interest on both the initial investment and the accumulated interest over time. It allows your investments to grow exponentially as earnings generate additional returns.

b. Benefits of Compounding:

i. Snowball Effect: As your investment grows, the compounding effect accelerates, leading to significant wealth accumulation over time.

ii. Time is Your Ally: The longer your investment horizon, the greater the impact of compounding. Starting early and staying invested for the long term maximizes the benefits of compounding.

c. Harnessing the Power of Compounding:

i. Start Investing Early: The earlier you begin investing, the more time your investments have to compound and grow.

ii. Reinvest Dividends and Capital Gains: Instead of taking cash distributions, reinvest them to buy additional shares, harnessing the compounding effect.

iii. Maintain a Long-Term Perspective: Avoid frequent trading and short-term thinking, as it can disrupt the power of compounding. Stay committed to your long-term investment plan.

Combining Dollar-Cost Averaging and Compounding:

a. Synergistic Effects: When dollar-cost averaging and compounding work together, they create a powerful wealth-building mechanism. Consistently investing over time while benefiting from the compounding effect can yield substantial returns.

b. Long-Term Mindset: Both dollar-cost averaging and compounding require a long-term perspective. Embrace the journey of gradual accumulation and growth, understanding that wealth-building takes time and consistent effort.

c. Periodic Evaluation and Adjustments: Regularly review and assess your investment plan to ensure it remains aligned with your goals and financial circumstances. Make adjustments as necessary, considering changes in risk tolerance, time horizon, or financial objectives.

Dollar-cost averaging, and the power of compounding are potent tools that can accelerate your path to financial success. By consistently investing over time, irrespective of market conditions, and harnessing the compounding effect, you can build wealth and achieve your long-term financial goals. Embrace the discipline, patience, and long-term mindset required, and let the combined forces of dollar-cost averaging and compounding work in your favor.

CHAPTER SIX

Unleashing the Potential of Stock Market Investing: Navigating the Path to Wealth

Stock market investing has long been recognized as one of the most powerful wealth-building strategies. By owning shares in publicly traded companies, investors have the opportunity to participate in the growth and success of businesses. Now it's time to learn about stock market investing, covering key concepts, strategies, and considerations that can help you navigate this dynamic and potentially rewarding investment landscape.

Understanding Stocks and the Stock Market:

a. What are Stocks? Stocks represent ownership shares in a company. When you invest in stocks, you become a partial owner and can potentially benefit from the company's profits and growth.

b. The Stock Market: The stock market refers to the marketplace where buyers and sellers trade stocks. It provides a platform for investors to buy and sell shares, facilitated through stock exchanges such as the New York Stock Exchange (NYSE) or NASDAQ.

Key Concepts in Stock Market Investing:

a. Risk and Return: Stock market investing involves balancing risk and return. Stocks offer the potential for higher returns compared to other asset classes but also carry higher levels of volatility and risk.

b. Fundamental Analysis: Fundamental analysis involves assessing a company's financial health, competitive positioning, management team, and industry trends to determine the intrinsic value of its stock.

c. Technical Analysis: Technical analysis involves studying historical price and volume patterns to predict future stock price movements. It utilizes charts, trends, and indicators to make investment decisions.

d. Market Efficiency and Behavioral Finance: Understanding market efficiency and behavioral finance can provide insights into market dynamics, investor behavior, and potential opportunities for value investing or contrarian strategies.

Investment Strategies for Stock Market Investing:

a. Long-Term Investing: Adopting a long-term investment approach involves holding stocks for an extended period, aiming to benefit from the compounding effect and the growth potential of solid companies.

b. Value Investing: Value investors seek stocks that are undervalued relative to their intrinsic value. They focus on companies with solid fundamentals but are trading at a discount, offering the potential for capital appreciation.

c. Growth Investing: Growth investors seek stocks of companies with strong growth potential. They look for companies that demonstrate high earnings growth rates, innovation, and expansion opportunities.

d. Dividend Investing: Dividend investors prioritize stocks of companies that consistently pay dividends. They seek regular income streams and potential dividend growth over time.

e. Index Investing and Exchange-Traded Funds (ETFs): Index investing involves investing in a broad market index, such as the S&P 500, to achieve broad market exposure. ETFs are investment funds that trade on stock exchanges and aim to replicate the performance of specific indexes or sectors.

Risks and Considerations:

a. Market Volatility: Stock prices can experience significant fluctuations due to market conditions, economic factors, or company-specific events. Understand and be prepared for market volatility.

b. Diversification: Diversifying your stock portfolio across different companies, sectors, and regions can help mitigate risk. Avoid overconcentration in a single stock or sector.

c. Research and Due Diligence: Conduct thorough research and due diligence before investing in stocks. Evaluate company financials, industry trends, management quality, and competitive positioning.

d. Emotional Discipline: Emotional discipline is crucial in stock market investing. Avoid making impulsive decisions based on short-term market movements or succumbing to herd mentality.

Investor Resources and Tools:

a. Financial News and Analysis: Stay informed about market news, company earnings releases, and economic indicators that may impact stock prices. Utilize reputable financial news sources and analysis platforms.

b. Online Brokers and Trading Platforms: Choose an online broker or trading platform that offers user-friendly interfaces, research tools, real-time data, and competitive trading fees.

c. Investor Education: Continuously educate yourself about stock market investing through books, online courses, seminars, and financial literacy resources.

Stock market investing offers tremendous potential for wealth accumulation and participation in the growth of companies. By understanding the key concepts, strategies, and considerations outlined in this chapter, you can embark on a rewarding journey in stock market investing. Remember to conduct thorough research, maintain a long-term perspective, and approach the stock market with discipline, patience, and a well-diversified portfolio. With diligent effort and informed decision-making, you can harness the power of stock market investing to achieve your financial goals.

Fundamental Analysis and Company Valuation: Unveiling the Inner Workings of Stocks

Fundamental analysis and company valuation are essential tools for investors seeking to make informed investment decisions in the stock market. By delving into a company's financial health, competitive position, and growth prospects, fundamental analysis enables investors to assess the intrinsic value of a stock. In this chapter, we will explore the intricacies of fundamental analysis and company valuation, equipping you with the knowledge and skills to evaluate stocks based on their underlying fundamentals.

Understanding Fundamental Analysis:

a. What is Fundamental Analysis? Fundamental analysis is a method of evaluating stocks by examining the underlying financial and qualitative factors of a company. It involves analyzing a company's financial statements, industry dynamics, competitive positioning, and management quality.

b. Key Components of Fundamental Analysis:

i. Financial Statements: Analyze a company's financial statements, including the balance sheet, income statement, and cash flow statement, to assess its financial performance, liquidity, and solvency.

ii. Ratio Analysis: Utilize financial ratios, such as price-to-earnings (P/E), price-to-sales (P/S), and return on equity (ROE), to compare a company's financial performance against industry benchmarks and peers.

iii. Qualitative Factors: Consider qualitative aspects such as the company's competitive advantages, market share, brand reputation, management team, and industry trends to evaluate its long-term prospects.

iv. Industry and Market Analysis: Assess the company's position within its industry, market trends, and potential growth drivers or risks that could impact its future performance.

Valuation Methods:

a. Discounted Cash Flow (DCF) Analysis: DCF analysis estimates the intrinsic value of a company by projecting its future cash flows and discounting them back to the present value. This method focuses on the company's ability to generate cash flows over time.

b. Price-to-Earnings (P/E) Ratio: The P/E ratio compares a company's stock price to its earnings per share (EPS). It provides insights into the market's valuation of the company relative to its earnings.

c. Price-to-Book (P/B) Ratio: The P/B ratio compares a company's stock price to its book value per share. It measures the market's valuation of a company's assets relative to its share price.

d. Dividend Discount Model (DDM): DDM estimates the intrinsic value of a company's stock based on the present value of its expected future dividend payments.

e. Comparable Company Analysis: In this method, analysts compare the valuation multiples of a target company to those of similar companies in the industry. It provides a relative valuation perspective.

Conducting Fundamental Analysis:

a. Financial Statement Analysis: Review a company's financial statements, focusing on revenue growth, profitability, debt levels, liquidity, and operating efficiency. Analyze trends and assess the company's ability to generate sustainable earnings and cash flows.

b. Industry Analysis: Evaluate the industry dynamics, market share, competitive landscape, and growth prospects. Consider macroeconomic factors and industry-specific trends that may impact the company's performance.

c. Management Assessment: Assess the quality and track record of the company's management team. Look for effective leadership, strategic vision, and transparent communication with shareholders.

d. SWOT Analysis: Conduct a SWOT (Strengths, Weaknesses, Opportunities, Threats) analysis to identify the company's internal strengths and weaknesses and external opportunities and threats.

Limitations and Risks:

a. Inherent Uncertainty: Fundamental analysis involves making assumptions and forecasts based on available information. The future performance of a company may deviate from projections, introducing uncertainty.

b. Data Limitations: Financial statements and data can be subject to manipulation or errors. It is essential to verify the accuracy and reliability of the information used for analysis.

c. Market Efficiency: The stock market may already reflect the available information, making it challenging to find undervalued or overvalued stocks solely through fundamental analysis.

Fundamental analysis and company valuation are powerful tools that allow investors to assess the underlying worth of a stock based on a company's financial health, industry position, and growth potential. By applying diligent research and analysis techniques, you can make informed investment decisions and identify opportunities for long-term wealth creation. However, it's crucial to recognize the limitations and risks associated with fundamental analysis and supplement it with other forms of analysis and market insights. Through continuous learning and refinement of your fundamental analysis skills, you can enhance your ability to identify promising investment opportunities in the stock market.

Unleashing the Power of Technical Analysis and Market Timing: Navigating the Dynamic Terrain of Stock Market Trends

Technical analysis and market timing are approaches utilized by traders and investors to analyze past price movements, identify patterns, and make predictions about future stock market trends.

While fundamental analysis focuses on the intrinsic value of a company, technical analysis examines historical price and volume data to forecast short-term price movements. In this section, we will learn the concepts and techniques of technical analysis and market timing, providing insights into their applications, benefits, and considerations.

Understanding Technical Analysis:

a. What is Technical Analysis? Technical analysis involves studying historical price patterns, chart patterns, and trading indicators to forecast future price movements. It is based on the belief that historical market data can provide insights into future trends and market behavior.

b. Key Components of Technical Analysis:

i. Price Patterns: Identify recurring patterns in stock prices, such as trends (uptrends, downtrends), reversals, consolidations, and breakouts. Common chart patterns include head and shoulders, double tops/bottoms, and triangles.

ii. Technical Indicators: Use mathematical calculations applied to price and volume data to generate trading signals. Examples of technical indicators include moving averages, relative strength index (RSI), stochastic oscillators, and Bollinger Bands.

iii. Support and Resistance Levels: Determine key levels where buying or selling pressure historically has caused prices to reverse or stall. Support levels are price levels where buying is expected to emerge, while resistance levels are price levels where selling pressure tends to be strong.

Market Timing:

a. What is Market Timing? Market timing refers to the practice of attempting to predict the future direction of stock markets or individual stocks to buy or sell at advantageous times. It involves making decisions based on technical analysis signals, economic indicators, or other timing models.

b. Approaches to Market Timing:

i. Trend-Following: Identify and ride the established trends in the market, aiming to capture gains during uptrends and exit positions during downtrends.

ii. Contrarian Strategies: Take positions opposite to prevailing market sentiment. Contrarian investors may buy when others are selling (at market bottoms) or sell when others are buying (at market tops).

iii. Momentum Investing: Capitalize on stocks or sectors with strong recent price momentum. Momentum investors buy stocks that are performing well and sell those with weak performance.

Benefits and Considerations of Technical Analysis and Market Timing:

a. Benefits of Technical Analysis:

i. Short-Term Trading Opportunities: Technical analysis is well-suited for short-term traders seeking to profit from short-lived price movements and volatility.

ii. Visual Representation of Market Trends: Charts provide a visual representation of historical price patterns and trends, facilitating the identification of potential trading opportunities.

iii. Timing Entries and Exits: Technical analysis can help determine optimal entry and exit points for trades, potentially enhancing trading performance.

b. Considerations and Risks:

i. Limitations of Predictive Power: Technical analysis is not foolproof and cannot guarantee accurate predictions. It is subject to false signals, market manipulation, and external factors that may override technical patterns.

ii. Emotional Discipline: Effective technical analysis requires emotional discipline to follow trading strategies and avoid impulsive decisions based on short-term price movements.

iii. Complementary Analysis: Technical analysis should be used in conjunction with other forms of analysis, such as fundamental analysis, to obtain a comprehensive view of investments.

Technical Analysis Tools and Resources:

a. Charting Software: Utilize charting platforms and software that provide a wide range of technical indicators, drawing tools, and customization options.

b. Education and Research: Continuously learn and stay updated on technical analysis techniques, attend webinars, read books, and follow reputable technical analysts and resources.

Technical analysis and market timing offer valuable tools for traders and investors seeking to capitalize on short-term price movements and identify potential trading opportunities. By understanding the key concepts and techniques of technical analysis, you can enhance your ability to read charts, identify patterns, and make informed trading decisions. However, it is important to recognize the limitations and risks associated with technical analysis, as it is not a guaranteed method for predicting market movements. Remember to supplement technical analysis with other forms of analysis and maintain emotional discipline while executing trading strategies. With practice, education, and a well-rounded approach, you can harness the power of technical analysis and market timing to potentially enhance your trading performance in the dynamic landscape of the stock market.

Diversification and Portfolio Management: Building Resilient Investment Portfolios

Diversification is a fundamental principle of portfolio management that aims to reduce risk and enhance returns by spreading investments across different asset classes, industries, and geographical regions. By constructing a well-diversified investment portfolio, investors can achieve a balance between risk and reward. Let us delve into the concept of diversification and explore portfolio management strategies that can help optimize investment outcomes.

Understanding Diversification:

a. What is Diversification? Diversification involves spreading investments across a variety of assets to mitigate the impact of individual investment risks. The objective is to build a portfolio that is not overly reliant on any single investment or asset class.

b. Benefits of Diversification:

i. Risk Reduction: Diversification helps reduce the impact of individual security or sector-specific risks on the overall portfolio by distributing investments across different assets.

ii. Enhancing Returns: Diversification can potentially enhance returns by allocating investments to different asset classes or industries that may perform well in different market conditions.

iii. Smoothing Portfolio Volatility: Diversified portfolios tend to experience smoother and more stable returns over time, reducing the impact of market fluctuations.

Asset Allocation:

a. Strategic Asset Allocation: Strategic asset allocation refers to the long-term allocation of investments across different asset classes based on an investor's risk tolerance, financial goals, and time horizon. It sets the foundation for a diversified portfolio.

b. Tactical Asset Allocation: Tactical asset allocation involves adjusting the portfolio's asset allocation in response to short-term market conditions or changing economic outlooks. It aims to capitalize on short-term market opportunities or mitigate risks.

c. Rebalancing: Rebalancing involves periodically realigning the portfolio's asset allocation to maintain the desired risk and return profile. It involves selling overperforming assets and buying underperforming assets to bring the portfolio back to its target allocation.

Portfolio Diversification Strategies:

a. Asset Class Diversification: Allocate investments across different asset classes, such as stocks, bonds, cash, and alternative investments, to capture the unique risk-return characteristics of each asset class.

b. Sector and Industry Diversification: Spread investments across various sectors and industries to reduce concentration risk. This ensures that the portfolio is not overly exposed to the performance of a specific sector.

c. Geographical Diversification: Invest in different regions and countries to benefit from global economic growth and reduce the impact of regional-specific risks.

d. Investment Style Diversification: Diversify investments across different investment styles, such as value, growth, or income-oriented strategies, to capture opportunities across different market conditions.

e. Risk Management: Implement risk management techniques, such as including low-risk assets like bonds or incorporating hedging strategies, to protect the portfolio against adverse market movements.

Monitoring and Performance Evaluation:

a. Regular Portfolio Review: Conduct periodic reviews of the portfolio's performance, asset allocation, and individual investments to ensure alignment with investment objectives and make necessary adjustments.

b. Performance Metrics: Utilize performance metrics, such as portfolio return, risk-adjusted returns, and benchmark comparisons, to evaluate the portfolio's performance relative to its objectives and benchmarks.

c. Tax Efficiency: Consider the tax implications of portfolio management decisions and implement tax-efficient strategies, such as tax-loss harvesting or utilizing tax-advantaged accounts, to optimize after-tax returns.

Diversification and portfolio management are crucial components of successful investing. By diversifying across asset classes, sectors, geographies, and investment styles, investors can reduce risk, enhance returns, and achieve a balanced portfolio. Implementing an appropriate asset allocation strategy, regularly monitoring the portfolio's performance, and making necessary adjustments based on changing market conditions and goals are essential for effective portfolio management.

Remember that diversification does not guarantee profits or protect against losses, but it can help manage risk and potentially improve long-term investment outcomes. By applying the principles of diversification and portfolio management, you can build a resilient and well-structured investment portfolio that aligns with your financial goals and risk tolerance.

Bonds and Fixed-Income Investments: An Essential Guide to Income Generation and Risk Management

Bonds and fixed-income investments play a vital role in investment portfolios by providing steady income, capital preservation, and diversification benefits. These investment vehicles are popular among investors seeking stable returns and a more conservative approach to wealth building. It's time to understand the basics of bonds and fixed-income investments, their characteristics, and the considerations for investors looking to incorporate them into their investment strategy.

Understanding Bonds:

a. What are Bonds? Bonds are debt instruments issued by governments, municipalities, corporations, and other entities to raise capital. When an investor buys a bond, they are essentially lending money to the issuer in exchange for periodic interest payments (coupon) and the return of the principal amount at maturity.

b. Bond Characteristics:

i. Coupon Rate: The coupon rate is the fixed interest rate paid by the issuer to bondholders annually or semi-annually, expressed as a percentage of the bond's face value.

ii. Maturity: The maturity is the specified date on which the bond's principal is repaid to the bondholder. Bonds can have short-term (less than one year), intermediate-term (one to ten years), or long-term (greater than ten years) maturities.

iii. Credit Rating: Credit rating agencies assess the creditworthiness of bond issuers and assign ratings that reflect the issuer's ability to repay the bond's principal and interest.

Higher-rated bonds are generally considered less risky.

iv. Yield: The yield represents the effective return on a bond, taking into account the bond's price and coupon payments. Yields can be influenced by factors such as prevailing interest rates, credit quality, and market conditions.

Types of Bonds:

a. Government Bonds: Issued by national governments, these bonds are considered low-risk due to the backing of the government's taxing authority. Examples include U.S. Treasury bonds, UK Gilts, and German Bunds.

b. Corporate Bonds: Issued by corporations to finance their operations or expansion. Corporate bonds offer varying levels of risk and return based on the issuer's creditworthiness and the bond's rating.

c. Municipal Bonds: Issued by state and local governments to fund public infrastructure projects. Municipal bonds often offer tax advantages and can be attractive to investors in higher tax brackets.

d. Treasury Inflation-Protected Securities (TIPS): These bonds are specifically designed to protect against inflation by adjusting their principal value based on changes in the Consumer Price Index (CPI).

e. High-Yield Bonds: Also known as junk bonds, these bonds are issued by companies with lower credit ratings and, consequently, offer higher yields to compensate for the increased risk.

Benefits of Bonds and Fixed-Income Investments:

a. Income Generation: Bonds provide a predictable stream of income through regular coupon payments, making them particularly appealing to income-oriented investors seeking steady cash flow.

b. Capital Preservation: High-quality bonds are generally considered less volatile than stocks, providing a level of capital preservation and stability to investment portfolios.

c. Diversification: Bonds offer diversification benefits by having a low or negative correlation with equities. When combined with other asset classes, such as stocks, bonds can help reduce overall portfolio risk.

d. Risk Management: Fixed-income investments, particularly high-quality bonds, can act as a cushion during periods of market volatility and economic downturns, helping to offset potential losses in riskier assets.

Considerations for Bond Investors:

a. Yield and Risk Trade-Off: Higher yields often come with increased risk. Investors should carefully assess the creditworthiness of the bond issuer and consider the potential impact of changing interest rates on bond prices.

b. Duration and Interest Rate Sensitivity: Duration measures the sensitivity of a bond's price to changes in interest rates. Longer-duration bonds are generally more sensitive to interest rate movements, which can impact their market value.

c. Diversification: Investors should diversify their bond holdings by considering a mix of different issuers, maturities, and credit ratings to manage risks and optimize returns.

d. Tax Considerations: Different bonds may have varying tax implications. Municipal bonds, for example, may offer tax advantages, while some government bonds may be subject to federal income tax.

Bonds and fixed-income investments offer investors the opportunity to generate income, preserve capital, and diversify their portfolios. By understanding the basics of bonds, including their characteristics, types, and benefits, investors can make informed decisions about incorporating fixed-income investments into their overall investment strategy. It is essential to carefully assess the creditworthiness of issuers, consider interest rate sensitivity, and diversify holdings to manage risk effectively. Bonds can be valuable tools for income generation and risk management, providing stability and balance to investment portfolios.

Exploring the Types of Bonds: Characteristics and Considerations

Bonds are popular investment vehicles known for their stability, income generation, and diversification benefits. They come in various types, each with its own unique characteristics and considerations. In this section, we will review the different types of bonds, their key features, and factors to consider when investing in them.

Government Bonds:

Government bonds are issued by national governments and are considered low-risk investments due to the backing of the government's taxing authority. They are often used to finance government expenditures and infrastructure projects. Here are some common types of government bonds:

a. Treasury Bonds: Issued by the government to fund its operations, treasury bonds have longer maturities ranging from 10 to 30 years. They offer fixed interest payments and return the principal amount at maturity.

b. Treasury Notes: These are medium-term government bonds with maturities ranging from 1 to 10 years. They provide regular interest payments and return the principal at maturity.

c. Treasury Bills: Short-term government bonds with maturities of less than 1 year, treasury bills are typically issued at a discount to their face value and do not pay periodic interest. Instead, investors earn the difference between the purchase price and the face value at maturity.

Corporate Bonds:

Corporate bonds are issued by corporations to raise capital for various purposes, such as expansion, acquisitions, or debt refinancing. They offer higher yields than government bonds but carry varying levels of credit risk. Some types of corporate bonds include:

a. Investment-Grade Bonds: These bonds are issued by companies with strong credit ratings, indicating a lower risk of default. They tend to offer lower yields compared to riskier bonds.

b. High-Yield Bonds (Junk Bonds): High-yield bonds are issued by companies with lower credit ratings. They carry higher default risk but offer higher yields to compensate investors for taking on additional risk.

c. Convertible Bonds: Convertible bonds give bondholders the option to convert their bonds into a predetermined number of the issuer's common stock. They offer potential upside through equity participation along with the regular coupon payments.

Municipal Bonds:

Municipal bonds, or "munis," are issued by state and local governments, as well as government agencies, to finance public infrastructure projects. They offer income that is often exempt from federal income tax and can be categorized into two main types:

a. General Obligation Bonds: Backed by the full faith and credit of the issuing municipality, general obligation bonds are secured by the municipality's taxing authority. They have a lower risk of default but may offer lower yields.

b. Revenue Bonds: Revenue bonds are backed by the revenue generated from specific projects or facilities, such as toll roads, airports, or utilities. They carry higher default risk but may offer higher yields compared to general obligation bonds.

International Bonds:

International bonds are issued by foreign governments, corporations, or supranational entities. They provide exposure to global markets and can diversify a portfolio. Some common types include:

a. Sovereign Bonds: Issued by foreign governments, sovereign bonds carry varying levels of credit risk depending on the issuing country's financial stability and creditworthiness.

b. Foreign Corporate Bonds: These bonds are issued by foreign corporations and can provide opportunities to invest in specific industries or regions outside of one's home country.

Understanding the different types of bonds and their characteristics is crucial for building a diversified and balanced investment portfolio. Government bonds offer low-risk options, while corporate bonds provide higher yields with varying levels of credit risk. Municipal bonds can offer tax advantages, and international bonds provide exposure to global markets. Investors should carefully evaluate the credit quality, duration, and yield of bonds, as well as consider their risk tolerance and investment objectives when selecting bonds for their portfolio. By diversifying across different bond types, investors can effectively manage risk and generate income within their investment strategy.

Bond Yield Calculations and Understanding Interest Rate Risk

Bond yield calculations and understanding interest rate risk are essential aspects of bond investing. Bond yields provide insight into the potential returns of a bond investment, while interest rate risk helps investors assess the impact of changes in interest rates on bond prices. In this chapter, we will learn how to calculate bond yields and delve into the concept of interest rate risk.

Calculating Bond Yields:

a. Coupon Yield: The coupon yield represents the annual interest payment as a percentage of the bond's face value. It is calculated by dividing the annual coupon payment by the face value of the bond.

b. Current Yield: The current yield is calculated by dividing the annual coupon payment by the current market price of the bond. It provides a more accurate measure of the bond's yield relative to its current market value.

c. Yield to Maturity (YTM): YTM is a comprehensive measure of a bond's total return if held until maturity. It considers the coupon payments, the bond's purchase price, and the principal repayment at maturity. YTM takes into account the time value of money and is calculated using complex mathematical formulas. Investors can use online calculators or financial software to determine YTM.

Understanding Interest Rate Risk:

a. Definition: Interest rate risk refers to the potential impact of changes in interest rates on the value of a bond. When interest rates rise, existing bonds with lower coupon rates become less attractive to investors, leading to a decrease in their market value. Conversely, when interest rates decline, existing bonds with higher coupon rates may become more valuable.

b. Factors Influencing Interest Rate Risk:

i. Bond Maturity: Longer-term bonds generally have higher interest rate risk than shorter-term bonds because changes in interest rates have a more significant impact on future cash flows.

ii. Coupon Rate: Bonds with fixed coupon rates are more susceptible to interest rate risk than floating-rate bonds, which adjust their coupon payments based on prevailing interest rates.

iii. Yield Curve: The shape of the yield curve can affect interest rate risk. A steeper yield curve implies greater interest rate uncertainty, while a flatter curve indicates more stability.

c. Managing Interest Rate Risk:

i. Diversification: Spreading investments across bonds with varying maturities and interest rate risk profiles can help mitigate the impact of interest rate fluctuations on the overall portfolio.

ii. Bond Laddering: Bond laddering involves investing in bonds with staggered maturities. This strategy helps reduce reinvestment risk and provides flexibility to take advantage of changing interest rate environments.

iii. Duration: Duration measures a bond's sensitivity to changes in interest rates. By selecting bonds with shorter durations, investors can reduce interest rate risk.

Yield Curve and Yield Spread Analysis:

a. Yield Curve: The yield curve is a graphical representation of interest rates for bonds with varying maturities. It helps investors assess the relationship between bond yields and their corresponding maturities. The yield curve can be upward-sloping (normal), flat, or inverted, indicating different expectations for future interest rates.

b. Yield Spread Analysis: Yield spreads refer to the difference in yields between different types of bonds or credit qualities. Investors analyze yield spreads to assess relative value and credit risk. Widening spreads may indicate increased market uncertainty or deteriorating credit conditions, while narrowing spreads may suggest improving market conditions.

Understanding bond yield calculations and interest rate risk is crucial for bond investors. Bond yields provide insight into potential returns, while interest rate risk helps assess the impact of interest rate changes on bond prices. By calculating bond yields accurately and considering interest rate risk factors, investors can make informed decisions and manage their bond portfolios effectively. Diversification, bond laddering, and duration analysis are strategies that can help mitigate interest rate risk and optimize bond investment outcomes.

Real Estate Investing: Building Wealth through Property

Real estate investing is a popular wealth-building strategy that offers the potential for long-term appreciation, rental income, tax advantages, and diversification. Let's uncover the fundamentals of real estate investing, including different investment approaches, considerations, and key factors to help you navigate the world of real estate.

Types of Real Estate Investments:

a. Residential Properties: Residential properties, such as single-family homes, condominiums, and multi-unit apartment buildings, are commonly sought after by investors. These properties can generate rental income and benefit from potential property value appreciation.

b. Commercial Properties: Commercial real estate encompasses office buildings, retail spaces, industrial properties, and warehouses. Investing in commercial properties often involves leasing to businesses and can provide steady rental income.

c. Real Estate Investment Trusts (REITs): REITs are investment vehicles that pool capital from multiple investors to invest in various types of real estate properties. They offer a convenient way to access real estate markets and provide liquidity.

d. Real Estate Development: Real estate development involves purchasing land and constructing properties for sale or rent. This approach requires in-depth knowledge of local markets, construction processes, and potential risks.

Key Considerations for Real Estate Investors:

a. Market Analysis: Evaluating local real estate markets is crucial to identify areas with growth potential, rental demand, and favorable economic conditions. Factors such as population growth, job market, and infrastructure development can impact property values.

b. Financing Options: Understanding financing options is essential when investing in real estate. Consider traditional bank loans, private lenders, or creative financing methods to acquire properties while managing cash flow and maximizing returns.

c. Risk Assessment: Real estate investing involves various risks, including market fluctuations, property vacancies, unexpected maintenance costs, and regulatory changes. Conducting thorough due diligence, performing property inspections, and assessing potential risks are vital steps.

d. Property Management: Effective property management is crucial for rental properties. Consider whether self-management or hiring a professional property management company aligns with your goals and resources.

Benefits and Strategies of Real Estate Investing:

a. Potential Appreciation: Real estate has historically shown appreciation over the long term. Strategic property selection, location, and market timing can contribute to potential property value growth.

b. Rental Income: Rental properties offer a steady income stream from monthly rental payments. Analyze rental market trends, consider property expenses, and aim for positive cash flow to generate passive income.

c. Tax Advantages: Real estate investors can benefit from tax advantages, including deductions for mortgage interest, property taxes, depreciation, and expenses related to property management.

d. Diversification: Real estate can provide diversification benefits to an investment portfolio, as it tends to have a low correlation with other asset classes, such as stocks and bonds.

Risk Management in Real Estate Investing:

a. Cash Flow Analysis: Conduct thorough cash flow analysis to ensure rental income covers expenses, such as mortgage payments, property taxes, insurance, maintenance, and vacancies.

b. Property Inspections: Perform property inspections and due diligence to identify potential issues, assess the property's condition, and estimate maintenance or repair costs.

c. Adequate Insurance Coverage: Obtain appropriate insurance coverage to protect against potential liabilities, property damage, natural disasters, or unforeseen events.

d. Portfolio Diversification: Consider diversifying real estate investments across different property types, locations, and investment strategies to spread risk and enhance returns.

Real estate investing offers the potential for wealth accumulation through property appreciation, rental income, tax advantages, and portfolio diversification. Understanding the different types of real estate investments, conducting thorough market analysis, managing risks, and implementing effective strategies can help you navigate the real estate landscape and build a successful investment portfolio in this exciting asset class. Whether investing in residential properties, commercial real estate, REITs, or engaging in real estate development, align your investment approach with your financial goals and risk tolerance to maximize the potential benefits of real estate investing.

Investing in Rental Properties and Effective Property Management

Investing in rental properties can provide a reliable income stream, potential property appreciation, and long-term wealth accumulation. However, successful rental property investing goes beyond simply acquiring properties. So, what should be the key considerations and best practices for investing in rental properties and managing them effectively?

Property Selection and Acquisition:

a. Market Research: Conduct thorough market research to identify areas with strong rental demand, growth potential, and favorable economic conditions. Analyze factors such as population trends, employment opportunities, infrastructure development, and rental vacancy rates.

b. Property Evaluation: Assess potential rental properties based on their location, property type, condition, amenities, and potential rental income. Consider factors like proximity to amenities, schools, transportation, and the overall appeal to potential tenants.

c. Financial Analysis: Perform a comprehensive financial analysis, including estimating rental income, calculating expenses (e.g., mortgage payments, property taxes, insurance, maintenance costs), and projecting cash flow. Evaluate the potential return on investment (ROI) and ensure positive cash flow for sustainable income generation.

d. Financing and Property Acquisition: Explore financing options, such as traditional mortgages, private lenders, or partnerships, to acquire rental properties. Consider down payment requirements, interest rates, loan terms, and the impact on cash flow.

Effective Property Management:

a. Tenant Screening: Implement a thorough tenant screening process to select reliable and responsible tenants. Conduct background checks, verify employment and income, check references, and assess creditworthiness to reduce the risk of rental defaults or property damage.

b. Lease Agreements: Develop clear and comprehensive lease agreements that outline tenant responsibilities, rental terms, payment schedules, maintenance expectations, and dispute resolution procedures. Ensure compliance with local rental laws and regulations.

c. Maintenance and Repairs: Regularly inspect and maintain rental properties to ensure they are safe, functional, and attractive to tenants. Promptly address maintenance requests, handle repairs efficiently, and keep records of all maintenance activities.

d. Rent Collection and Financial Management: Establish an organized system for rent collection, including setting up secure payment methods and implementing policies for late payments. Keep accurate financial records, track income and expenses, and consider using property management software to streamline financial management.

e. Communication and Relationship Building: Foster positive relationships with tenants by maintaining open lines of communication, promptly addressing concerns or issues, and providing excellent customer service. This can lead to longer tenancies, reduced vacancies, and positive referrals.

f. Legal Compliance: Stay informed about local rental laws and regulations to ensure compliance with tenant rights, fair housing practices, safety standards, and property inspections. Consult legal professionals or property management experts for guidance if needed.

Risk Mitigation and Insurance:

a. Insurance Coverage: Obtain adequate insurance coverage for rental properties, including landlord insurance, liability insurance, and coverage for property damage, natural disasters, or unforeseen events. Regularly review and update insurance policies to ensure they align with property value and potential risks.

b. Emergency Planning: Develop contingency plans for emergencies, such as maintenance emergencies, tenant displacement, or unexpected events. Maintain a network of reliable contractors or service providers for quick response and resolution.

c. Legal Protection: Consult with legal professionals to understand landlord-tenant laws, eviction processes, and your rights and obligations as a landlord. Establish proper legal documentation and protocols to protect your interests and ensure compliance.

Investing in rental properties can be a rewarding and profitable venture when approached with diligence, strategic planning, and effective property management. Careful property selection, financial analysis, tenant screening, proactive maintenance, and compliance with legal requirements are crucial for successful rental property investing. By implementing sound property management practices, you can generate consistent rental income, mitigate risks, and build a portfolio of profitable rental properties.

Real Estate Investment Trusts (REITs): Accessing Real Estate Markets with Ease

Real Estate Investment Trusts (REITs) offer investors the opportunity to invest in real estate assets without the need for direct property ownership. REITs are investment vehicles that pool capital from multiple investors to invest in various types of real estate properties. In this chapter, we will explore the concept of REITs, their benefits, considerations, and key factors to help you understand and evaluate these investment options.

What are REITs?

a. Definition: A REIT is a company or trust that owns, operates, or finances income-generating real estate properties. REITs are required by law to distribute a significant portion of their taxable income as dividends to shareholders.

b. Types of REITs: REITs can be classified into various categories based on the types of properties they invest in, such as residential, commercial, industrial, retail, or specialized sectors like healthcare or hospitality.

c. Structure: REITs can be publicly traded on stock exchanges, known as publicly traded REITs, or privately held and not traded on exchanges, known as non-traded REITs. Publicly traded REITs provide liquidity and transparency, while non-traded REITs offer potential income and diversification benefits.

Benefits of Investing in REITs:

a. Diversification: REITs provide an opportunity to diversify investment portfolios by gaining exposure to a broad range of real estate properties and sectors.

b. Income Generation: REITs are required to distribute a significant portion of their taxable income as dividends, making them attractive for income-seeking investors.

c. Liquidity: Publicly traded REITs can be bought and sold on stock exchanges, offering investors the ability to easily enter or exit their investments.

d. Professional Management: REITs are managed by experienced real estate professionals who handle property acquisition, leasing, maintenance, and other operational aspects, reducing the burden of direct property management on individual investors.

e. Access to Large-Scale Properties: Investing in REITs allows individuals to gain exposure to high-value real estate assets that would typically require significant capital to acquire individually.

Considerations when investing in REITs:

a. Risk Factors: Like any investment, REITs carry certain risks. Market volatility, interest rate fluctuations, changes in property values, occupancy rates, and economic conditions can impact the performance of REITs.

b. Dividend Income and Tax Implications: REIT dividends are subject to specific tax rules and may be taxed differently than other forms of investment income. Investors should understand the tax implications of investing in REITs and consult with tax professionals.

c. Investment Objectives and Time Horizon: Consider your investment goals, risk tolerance, and time horizon when investing in REITs. Some REITs may offer higher potential returns but may also come with increased risk.

d. Due Diligence and Research: Conduct thorough research on the REIT's management team, historical performance, property portfolio, financials, and growth prospects. Review the prospectus or offering documents to understand the REIT's investment strategy and objectives.

Evaluating REITs:

a. Financial Metrics: Analyze key financial metrics such as funds from operations (FFO), net operating income (NOI), occupancy rates, debt levels, and dividend yields to assess the financial health and profitability of the REIT.

b. Property Portfolio Analysis: Evaluate the quality, diversity, location, and growth potential of the REIT's property portfolio. Consider factors such as occupancy rates, lease terms, tenant mix, and market demand for the property types the REIT invests in.

c. Management Team: Assess the expertise and track record of the REIT's management team. Look for experienced professionals with a successful history in real estate investing and asset management.

d. Regulatory Compliance: Ensure that the REIT complies with applicable laws, regulations, and reporting requirements. Review their filings with regulatory authorities to gain insights into their operations and adherence to industry standards.

Real Estate Investment Trusts (REITs) provide a convenient and accessible way for investors to gain exposure to the real estate market without direct property ownership. By investing in REITs, individuals can diversify their portfolios, generate income through dividend distributions, and benefit from professional management of real estate assets. However, it is important to carefully evaluate REITs, understand their risks, consider investment objectives, and conduct thorough research to make informed investment decisions.

Exploring Alternative Investment Opportunities: Precious Metals, Cryptocurrencies, and More

While traditional investments such as stocks and bonds form the foundation of many portfolios, alternative investment opportunities have gained popularity in recent years. These investments offer diversification, potential for high returns, and exposure to unique asset classes. In this chapter, we will explore several alternative investment options, including precious metals, cryptocurrencies, peer-to-peer lending, and venture capital.

Precious Metals:

a. Gold: Gold has long been considered a store of value and a hedge against inflation. Investors can purchase physical gold in the form of bars or coins or invest in gold-backed exchange-traded funds (ETFs) and mutual funds.

b. Silver: Silver is another precious metal that offers potential investment opportunities. It is used in various industries, including electronics, solar panels, and jewelry. Investors can purchase physical silver or invest in silver-focused ETFs.

c. Platinum and Palladium: Platinum and palladium are used extensively in the automotive and jewelry industries. These metals can also be purchased in physical form or invested in through ETFs and other investment vehicles.

Cryptocurrencies:

a. Bitcoin: Bitcoin, the first and most well-known cryptocurrency, has gained significant attention in recent years. It operates on a decentralized network and offers potential for high returns, but it also comes with increased volatility and risks.

b. Ethereum: Ethereum is a blockchain-based platform that supports the creation of smart contracts and decentralized applications (DApps). Its native cryptocurrency, Ether, has gained popularity for its utility within the Ethereum ecosystem.

c. Altcoins: Altcoins refer to cryptocurrencies other than Bitcoin and Ethereum. There are thousands of altcoins with varying features, use cases, and investment potential. It's essential to conduct thorough research before investing in any specific altcoin.

Peer-to-Peer Lending:

a. Peer-to-peer (P2P) lending platforms connect borrowers directly with lenders, eliminating the need for traditional financial institutions. Investors can earn interest by lending money to individuals or small businesses through online platforms.

b. P2P Real Estate Investing: Some platforms specialize in P2P real estate lending, allowing investors to fund real estate projects and earn returns based on interest payments or profit-sharing arrangements.

Venture Capital:

a. Venture capital (VC) involves investing in early-stage companies with high growth potential. VC investments are typically made in exchange for equity ownership in the company. This investment avenue requires thorough due diligence, as it comes with higher risks but can offer substantial returns.

b. Crowdfunding: Crowdfunding platforms allow individuals to invest in startups or small businesses with relatively small amounts of capital. It provides an opportunity to diversify investments across various companies and industries.

Collectibles and Art:

a. Collectibles: Collectibles, such as rare coins, stamps, vintage cars, and sports memorabilia, can appreciate in value over time. Investing in collectibles requires specialized knowledge and understanding of the market.

b. Art: Investing in art can offer potential returns and diversification. Artworks from renowned artists have historically shown appreciation, but this market can be subjective and illiquid. Seek advice from art experts before making significant art investments.

Alternative investments provide opportunities for diversification, potentially high returns, and exposure to unique asset classes beyond traditional investments. Precious metals, cryptocurrencies, peer-to-peer lending, venture capital, and collectibles are just a few examples of alternative investment options available to investors. It's important to thoroughly research and understand the risks and potential rewards associated with these investments, as well as consider their suitability within your overall investment strategy and risk tolerance.

CHAPTER SEVEN

Strategies for Successful Investing: Building a Solid Investment Approach

Successful investing requires a thoughtful and disciplined approach that aligns with your financial goals, risk tolerance, and time horizon. Let's understand key strategies and principles that can help you navigate the investment landscape and increase your chances of achieving long-term success.

Set Clear Financial Goals:

a. Define your financial goals: Determine your short-term and long-term financial objectives, such as retirement planning, saving for a down payment on a house, or funding a child's education. Setting clear goals helps guide your investment decisions and provides a benchmark for measuring progress.

b. Establish a timeline: Identify the time horizon for each goal.

Short-term goals may require more conservative investments, while long-term goals can benefit from a more growth-oriented approach.

Develop a Diversification Strategy:

a. Asset Allocation: Allocate your investment portfolio across different asset classes, such as stocks, bonds, real estate, and alternative investments. Diversification helps reduce risk by spreading your investments across various sectors and asset types.

b. Risk Management: Consider your risk tolerance when determining your asset allocation. A conservative investor may prefer a higher allocation to bonds and cash, while an aggressive investor may have a higher allocation to stocks and alternative investments.

c. Rebalance Regularly: Periodically review your portfolio and rebalance it to maintain your desired asset allocation. Rebalancing ensures that your portfolio stays aligned with your investment objectives and helps manage risk.

Embrace a Long-Term Perspective:

a. Avoid Market Timing: Trying to time the market is challenging and often results in missed opportunities. Instead, adopt a long-term perspective and focus on the fundamentals of your investments.

b. Stay Disciplined: Stick to your investment plan and avoid making emotional decisions based on short-term market fluctuations. Consistent and disciplined investing over the long term tends to yield better results.

Conduct Thorough Research and Due Diligence:

a. Fundamental Analysis: When investing in individual stocks or bonds, conduct thorough fundamental analysis. Evaluate factors such as financial health, competitive position, industry trends, and management quality to make informed investment decisions.

b. Risk Assessment: Assess the risks associated with each investment, including market risk, credit risk, and liquidity risk. Understand the potential rewards and risks before committing capital.

c. Seek Professional Advice: Consider working with a financial advisor who can provide guidance, research, and expertise tailored to your investment goals and risk tolerance.

Stay Informed and Continuously Learn:

a. Stay Current: Keep abreast of market trends, economic indicators, and news that can impact your investments. Stay informed about the industries and sectors you invest in.

b. Expand Your Knowledge: Continuously educate yourself about investing concepts, strategies, and new investment opportunities. Attend seminars, read books, follow reputable financial publications, and engage in investment communities.

Regularly Monitor and Evaluate Performance:

a. Monitor Investments: Regularly review the performance of your investments and assess if they are meeting your expectations. Keep track of key metrics, such as return on investment, expenses, and risk-adjusted returns.

b. Adjust as Needed: If an investment consistently underperforms or no longer aligns with your goals, consider making changes to your portfolio. Be cautious of making impulsive decisions based on short-term performance.

Successful investing is a result of careful planning, discipline, and continuous learning. By setting clear financial goals, diversifying your portfolio, adopting a long-term perspective, conducting thorough research, and staying informed, you can build a solid investment strategy. Remember to regularly monitor and evaluate your investments and make adjustments as needed to stay on track toward achieving your financial objectives.

Long-Term Investing and the Power of Patience: Building Wealth Through Time

In today's fast-paced and information-driven investment landscape, it's easy to get caught up in short-term market fluctuations and the desire for quick gains. However, successful investing often requires a long-term perspective and the virtue of patience. Let's talk about the concept of long-term investing, its benefits, and why patience is a crucial attribute for building wealth over time.

Understanding Long-Term Investing:

Long-term investing is an investment approach focused on holding assets for an extended period, typically measured in years or even decades. It involves identifying fundamentally strong investments and allowing time and compounding to work in your favor.

The Benefits of Long-Term Investing:

a. Harnessing the Power of Compounding: Long-term investing allows you to benefit from the compounding effect, where your investment returns generate additional returns over time. The longer your investment horizon, the greater the potential for compounding to exponentially grow your wealth.

b. Riding Out Market Volatility: By taking a long-term approach, you can better withstand short-term market volatility and avoid making impulsive investment decisions based on temporary fluctuations. Over the long term, markets tend to trend upward, and short-term downturns can be smoothed out.

c. Minimizing Transaction Costs: Frequent buying and selling of investments can result in substantial transaction costs, such as brokerage fees and taxes. Long-term investing reduces the need for excessive trading, thereby minimizing costs and increasing overall investment returns.

The Importance of Patience in Long-Term Investing:

a. Embracing Time as an Ally: Patience is essential because it allows you to stay invested over the long term, enabling your investments to grow and generate substantial returns. It helps you avoid the temptation of chasing short-term market trends or reacting to daily market noise.

b. Overcoming Emotional Bias: Patience helps counteract emotional biases that can negatively impact investment decisions. It allows you to maintain discipline and avoid making impulsive moves driven by fear or greed, which can harm long-term investment performance.

c. Allowing Investments to Mature: Some investments take time to reach their full potential. Patience allows you to give your investments the necessary time to deliver the expected results, whether it's a business you've invested in or a long-term growth stock.

Strategies for Practicing Patience in Investing:

a. Develop a Long-Term Investment Plan: Set clear investment goals and establish a well-defined investment plan aligned with your financial objectives. A plan helps you stay focused on the long term and avoid succumbing to short-term market noise.

b. Adopt a Buy-and-Hold Approach: Identify high-quality investments and have confidence in their long-term prospects. Avoid the temptation to constantly trade or react to short-term market movements. Remember, successful investing is often a marathon, not a sprint.

c. Regularly Review and Rebalance: While long-term investing requires patience, it's important to review and rebalance your portfolio periodically. This helps ensure that your investments remain aligned with your goals and risk tolerance and allows for adjustments as needed.

Long-term investing and patience are intrinsically linked, with the potential to yield significant financial rewards over time. By maintaining a long-term perspective, harnessing the power of compounding, and exercising patience in decision-making, investors can build wealth steadily and withstand short-term market volatility. Remember, investing is a journey that rewards those who approach it with patience, discipline, and a focus on long-term success.

Regular Portfolio Review and Rebalancing: Maintaining Optimal Asset Allocation

Building an investment portfolio is just the first step toward achieving financial goals. To ensure continued alignment with your objectives and risk tolerance, it is crucial to regularly review and rebalance your portfolio. In this chapter, we will explore the importance of regular portfolio review, the process of rebalancing, and key considerations for maintaining an optimal asset allocation.

The Importance of Regular Portfolio Review:

a. Monitoring Performance: Regular portfolio review allows you to evaluate the performance of your investments, assess their alignment with your financial goals, and identify any underperforming assets or areas that require adjustments.

b. Staying Aligned with Goals: Financial goals may evolve over time due to life events, changing priorities, or market conditions. By conducting regular portfolio reviews, you can ensure your investments remain in sync with your objectives and make any necessary adjustments to maintain focus.

c. Risk Management: Markets fluctuate, and different asset classes may perform differently over time. Regular review enables you to assess the risk exposure of your portfolio and make adjustments to maintain an appropriate level of risk that aligns with your risk tolerance.

The Rebalancing Process:

a. Assessing Asset Allocation: Start by evaluating the current allocation of your portfolio across different asset classes such as stocks, bonds, real estate, and alternative investments. Determine whether any asset class has deviated significantly from your target allocation.

b. Identifying Deviations: Compare the current asset allocation to your target allocation. If an asset class has become over or underweight due to market movements, it may be necessary to rebalance the asset to bring it back to the desired allocation.

c. Setting Rebalancing Thresholds: Establish thresholds or triggers for rebalancing. For example, you may decide to rebalance if an asset class deviates by more than 5% from its target allocation.

This helps avoid excessive trading due to minor fluctuations.

d. Implementing Rebalancing: Rebalancing involves selling or buying assets to adjust their weightings. Sell overallocated assets and reinvest the proceeds into under-allocated assets to restore the desired asset allocation. Consider tax implications and transaction costs when executing rebalancing trades.

Considerations for Portfolio Review and Rebalancing:

a. Time Horizon and Risk Tolerance: Your time horizon and risk tolerance play a crucial role in determining the frequency and extent of portfolio review and rebalancing. Longer time horizons may allow for less frequent rebalancing, while shorter time horizons may require more active adjustments.

b. Changing Market Conditions: Market movements can impact the performance of different asset classes. Review economic indicators, market trends, and industry outlooks to assess how changing market conditions may affect your portfolio and rebalancing decisions.

c. Tax Efficiency: When rebalancing a taxable investment account, consider the potential tax consequences of selling assets. Explore tax-efficient strategies such as harvesting tax losses or utilizing tax-efficient investment vehicles to minimize tax liabilities.

d. Professional Guidance: Consider seeking guidance from a financial advisor or investment professional to help analyze your portfolio, provide objective insights, and offer personalized recommendations on rebalancing strategies based on your specific circumstances.

Regular portfolio review and rebalancing are essential components of successful portfolio management. By conducting periodic reviews, assessing asset allocation, and implementing rebalancing strategies, you can maintain an optimal allocation that aligns with your financial goals and risk tolerance. Stay informed, adapt to changing market conditions, and consider seeking professional guidance to ensure your portfolio remains on track for long-term success. Remember, portfolio review and rebalancing are ongoing processes that help you stay proactive and make informed investment decisions.

Tax-Efficient Investing Strategies: Maximizing Returns while Minimizing Tax Impact

Investing is not only about generating returns but also about managing the tax implications of your investments. Implementing tax-efficient investing strategies can help you minimize tax liabilities and maximize after-tax returns. Let's discuss various tax-efficient investment strategies to consider when building and managing your portfolio.

Understand Tax-Advantaged Accounts:

a. Retirement Accounts: Take full advantage of tax-advantaged retirement accounts such as 401(k)s, IRAs, or Roth IRAs. Contributions to these accounts may provide immediate tax benefits or tax-free growth, allowing you to defer taxes until withdrawal or potentially enjoy tax-free withdrawals in retirement.

b. Health Savings Accounts (HSAs): If eligible, contribute to an HSA, which offers triple tax advantages: tax-deductible contributions, tax-free growth, and tax-free withdrawals for qualified medical expenses. HSAs can serve as powerful long-term investment vehicles for healthcare expenses.

Asset Location and Asset Placement:

a. Tax-Efficient Asset Location: Consider the tax efficiency of different asset classes and allocate them strategically across taxable and tax-advantaged accounts. Tax-efficient investments, such as index funds or tax-managed mutual funds, may be more suitable for taxable accounts, while tax-inefficient investments, like actively managed funds, may be better placed in tax-advantaged accounts.

b. Tax-Aware Asset Placement: Similarly, consider the tax implications when deciding whether to hold certain investments in taxable or tax-advantaged accounts. Investments generating regular income, like bonds or REITs, are generally better suited for tax-advantaged accounts, while those with more long-term capital appreciation potential, such as stocks, may be more suitable for taxable accounts.

Harvest Tax Losses:

a. Tax Loss Harvesting: Offset capital gains by intentionally selling investments that have experienced a loss. The losses can be used to offset taxable gains, reducing your overall tax liability. Be mindful of tax rules and regulations surrounding wash sales, which prohibit buying a substantially identical investment within a specific timeframe.

b. Rebalance with Tax Efficiency in Mind: When rebalancing your portfolio, consider the tax implications of selling assets. Focus on selling investments with minimal gains to minimize taxable events while rebalancing your portfolio back to the desired asset allocation.

Utilize Tax-Efficient Investment Vehicles:

a. Index Funds and ETFs: Passively managed index funds and exchange-traded funds (ETFs) tend to generate fewer taxable events compared to actively managed funds. They typically have lower turnover rates, which can help reduce capital gains distributions and potential tax liabilities.

b. Tax-Managed Funds: Consider tax-managed mutual funds that aim to minimize taxable distributions. These funds employ strategies such as harvesting tax losses and focusing on long-term capital appreciation to help investors reduce tax consequences.

Timing and Strategies for Capital Gains:

a. Long-Term Capital Gains: Hold investments for more than one year to qualify for long-term capital gains tax rates, which are typically lower than short-term rates. This strategy can help minimize the tax impact when selling investments with significant gains.

b. Tax-Loss Carryforwards: If you have unused capital losses from previous years, you can carry them forward to offset future capital gains. This strategy can help reduce tax liabilities in years when gains are realized.

Seek Professional Guidance:

a. Consult with a Tax Advisor: Taxes can be complex, and the tax code is subject to change. Work with a tax advisor or accountant who specializes in investment taxation to navigate the complexities, understand your specific tax situation, and make informed decisions.

b. Consider a Financial Advisor: A financial advisor can help you develop and implement tax-efficient investment strategies tailored to your goals and circumstances. They can provide guidance on asset allocation, tax optimization, and ongoing portfolio management.

Implementing tax-efficient investing strategies can significantly impact your after-tax returns and help you keep more of your investment gains. By understanding tax-advantaged accounts, strategically locating assets, harvesting tax losses, utilizing tax-efficient investment vehicles, and considering timing strategies for capital gains, you can optimize your portfolio's tax efficiency. Remember to consult with tax and financial professionals to ensure the strategies align with your individual circumstances and stay informed about changes in tax laws. By incorporating tax efficiency into your investment approach, you can enhance your overall investment returns and work towards achieving your financial goals.

Dollar-Cost Averaging and Systematic Investing: Building Wealth through Consistent Contributions

Investing regularly and consistently is a key strategy for long-term wealth accumulation. Dollar-cost averaging, and systematic investing are two approaches that allow investors to contribute to their portfolios on a consistent basis, regardless of market conditions. Now, we will explore the concepts of dollar-cost averaging and systematic investing, their benefits, and how they can help you achieve your financial goals.

Understanding Dollar-Cost Averaging:

a. Definition: Dollar-cost averaging (DCA) is an investment strategy where you invest a fixed amount of money at regular intervals, regardless of the investment's price. This approach allows you to buy more shares when prices are low and fewer shares when prices are high.

b. Benefits of DCA:

-Reducing Market Timing Risk: DCA eliminates the need to time the market, as investments are made consistently over time. This helps mitigate the risk of investing a lump sum at the wrong time.

-Smoothing Out Market Volatility: By investing regularly, DCA helps average out the impact of market fluctuations, reducing the impact of short-term volatility on your overall investment performance.

-Disciplined Investing Approach: DCA encourages disciplined

investing behavior by setting a regular schedule for contributions. It helps remove emotions from investment decisions and promotes consistent long-term investing.

c. Example: Suppose you invest $500 per month in a particular stock. When prices are low, your $500 will buy more shares, and when prices are high, it will buy fewer shares. Over time, this averaging effect can potentially lead to favorable long-term returns.

Systematic Investing:

a. Definition: Systematic investing is a broader concept that encompasses various strategies, including dollar-cost averaging. It refers to consistently investing a fixed amount or a percentage of your income at regular intervals, such as monthly or quarterly.

b. Benefits of Systematic Investing:

-Automating Investment Contributions: By setting up automatic contributions, systematic investing ensures consistent investment without requiring active decision-making or manual interventions.

-Building a Habit of Savings and Investing: Systematic investing helps instill a habit of saving and investing regularly, making it easier to stay on track towards your financial goals.

-Mitigating Emotions and Behavioral Biases: Systematic investing reduces the impact of emotions and behavioral biases, such as fear or greed, which can lead to impulsive investment decisions.

c. Example: Setting up a monthly automated investment plan where a fixed amount is deducted from your bank account and invested in a diversified portfolio. This ensures that you consistently invest and benefit from the potential growth of your investments over time.

Considerations for Dollar-Cost Averaging and Systematic Investing:

a. Investment Horizon: Dollar-cost averaging, and systematic investing are ideally suited for long-term investment goals. The longer the investment horizon, the greater the potential benefits of these strategies.

b. Risk Tolerance: Assess your risk tolerance and align your investment strategy accordingly. DCA and systematic investing can help mitigate short-term volatility, but it's important to invest in line with your risk tolerance and financial objectives.

c. Cost Considerations: Be mindful of any transaction costs or fees associated with your investment accounts. Choose low-cost investment vehicles, such as index funds or ETFs, to minimize expenses and enhance your overall investment returns.

d. Regular Monitoring and Adjustment: While DCA and systematic investing are designed to be consistent and disciplined, it's still important to periodically review and adjust your investment strategy as needed to ensure it aligns with your changing goals and circumstances.

Dollar-cost averaging, and systematic investing are powerful strategies that promote consistency, discipline, and long-term wealth accumulation. By investing regularly, regardless of market conditions, you can mitigate timing risks, smooth out market volatility, and build wealth over time. Whether you choose to implement dollar-cost averaging or opt for a broader systematic investment approach, the key is to remain consistent, stay focused on your financial goals, and adjust your strategy as necessary. These strategies can help you navigate the ups and downs of the market and build a solid foundation for your financial future.

CHAPTER EIGHT

Mitigating Investment Risks: Strategies for a Resilient Portfolio

Investing inherently involves risks, but understanding and managing these risks is essential for building a resilient investment portfolio. In this chapter, we will explore various strategies and techniques to mitigate investment risks and increase the likelihood of achieving your financial goals.

Diversification:

a. Importance of Diversification: Diversification is a fundamental risk mitigation strategy that involves spreading investments across different asset classes, sectors, and geographical regions. By diversifying, you reduce the impact of any single investment or market event on your overall portfolio performance.

b. Asset Allocation: Allocate your portfolio across a mix of asset classes, such as stocks, bonds, real estate, and commodities, based on your risk tolerance, investment goals, and time horizon.

Diversifying across different asset classes can help balance risk and return potential.

c. Geographic and Sector Diversification: Consider diversifying investments across different countries and regions to reduce the risk of being overly exposed to the performance of a single economy. Additionally, diversify within sectors to avoid concentration risk in specific industries.

Risk Assessment and Risk Management:

a. Risk Assessment: Regularly evaluate the risks associated with your investments. Understand the risks specific to each asset class, such as market risk, credit risk, interest rate risk, and geopolitical risk. Conduct thorough research and analysis before making investment decisions.

b. Risk Management Techniques: Implement risk management techniques, such as setting stop-loss orders or utilizing hedging strategies, to protect your portfolio from significant downside risks. Consider using options, futures contracts, or other derivative instruments to hedge against adverse market movements.

Active Portfolio Monitoring and Rebalancing:

a. Regular Portfolio Monitoring: Stay informed about the performance of your investments and monitor any changes in market conditions. Review your portfolio periodically to ensure it aligns with your investment goals and risk tolerance.

b. Rebalancing: Rebalance your portfolio periodically to maintain your desired asset allocation. As different investments perform differently, rebalancing allows you to sell overperforming assets and buy underperforming assets, bringing your portfolio back in line with your intended risk exposure.

Investment Time Horizon and Long-Term Perspective:

a. Time Horizon Considerations: Align your investment strategy with your time horizon. Longer time horizons generally allow for greater tolerance of short-term market fluctuations. If you have a longer time horizon, you can afford to ride out market volatility and potentially benefit from the long-term growth of your investments.

b. Avoid Emotional Decision-Making: Emotions can lead to impulsive investment decisions. Stick to your investment plan, avoid making reactive changes based on short-term market movements, and maintain a long-term perspective.

Stay Informed and Seek Professional Advice:

a. Educate Yourself: Continuously educate yourself about different investment options, market trends, and economic indicators. Stay informed through reputable sources and consider attending investment seminars or workshops.

b. Consult with Professionals: Seek guidance from financial advisors or investment professionals who can provide personalized advice based on your financial goals, risk tolerance, and investment preferences. They can help you navigate complex investment landscapes and develop a customized risk mitigation strategy.

Mitigating investment risks is crucial for building a resilient portfolio that can withstand market fluctuations. By diversifying your investments, conducting thorough risk assessments, actively monitoring, and rebalancing your portfolio, considering your investment time horizon, and staying informed, you can navigate investment risks more effectively. Remember, no investment strategy can eliminate all risks, but by employing these strategies, you can reduce potential losses and increase the likelihood of achieving your financial goals over the long term.

Understanding Market Volatility and Emotional Investing: Staying Rational in a Roller-Coaster Market

Market volatility is an inherent characteristic of financial markets, and it can lead to emotional decision-making among investors. Understanding market volatility and learning how to manage emotions during turbulent times is crucial for successful investing. Now, we will delve into the nature of market volatility, its causes, and strategies for avoiding emotional investing pitfalls.

What is Market Volatility?

a. Definition: Market volatility refers to the magnitude and frequency of price fluctuations in financial markets. It is measured by indicators such as the volatility index (VIX) or standard deviation of returns.

b. Causes of Market Volatility: Market volatility can be attributed to various factors, including economic data releases, geopolitical events, changes in investor sentiment, market speculation, and unexpected news events. Understanding the drivers of volatility can help put market movements into perspective.

Emotional Investing and its Pitfalls:

a. Greed and Fear: Emotional investing is driven by two primary emotions: greed and fear. Greed leads investors to chase high returns without considering the associated risks, while fear prompts panic selling during market downturns.

b. Herd Mentality: Emotional investing often results from following the crowd. Investors may be influenced by the actions of others rather than conducting their own research and analysis.

c. Cognitive Biases: Investors are susceptible to cognitive biases, such as confirmation bias, recency bias, and loss aversion, which can cloud judgment and lead to irrational decision-making.

Strategies for Managing Emotional Investing:

a. Maintain a Long-Term Perspective: Understand that short-term market fluctuations are a normal part of investing. Focus on your long-term investment goals and avoid making impulsive decisions based on temporary market movements.

b. Develop an Investment Plan: Create a well-defined investment plan that aligns with your financial goals, risk tolerance, and time horizon. Having a plan in place provides a roadmap during volatile times and helps prevent emotional decision-making.

c. Conduct Thorough Research: Base investment decisions on sound research, analysis, and fundamental data. Thoroughly evaluate investment opportunities, considering factors such as company financials, industry trends, and economic indicators.

d. Diversify Your Portfolio: Diversification is a crucial risk management technique. Allocate your investments across different asset classes, sectors, and regions to spread risk and reduce the impact of individual investment performance on your portfolio.

e. Set Realistic Expectations: Understand that investing involves both ups and downs. Set realistic expectations about investment returns and be prepared for periods of volatility. Avoid chasing unrealistic gains and focus on long-term, sustainable growth.

f. Avoid Market Timing: Trying to time the market is a risky endeavor. Instead of attempting to buy at the lowest point or sell at the highest, focus on maintaining a consistent investment strategy and staying disciplined.

Market volatility and emotional investing often go hand in hand. However, by understanding the nature of market volatility, recognizing the pitfalls of emotional decision-making, and implementing strategies to manage emotions, you can navigate turbulent markets more effectively. By maintaining a long-term perspective, conducting thorough research, diversifying your portfolio, and seeking professional advice, you can make rational investment decisions that align with your financial goals and withstand market volatility. Remember, successful investing requires discipline, patience, and a focus on long-term outcomes.

Diversification and Asset Allocation: Building a Strong Investment Foundation

Diversification and asset allocation are two critical pillars of successful investing. By spreading investments across different asset classes, sectors, and geographical regions, investors can reduce risk and potentially enhance returns. Let's talk about the concepts of diversification and asset allocation, their benefits, and strategies for constructing a well-diversified portfolio.

Understanding Diversification:

a. Definition: Diversification is the strategy of allocating investments across a variety of assets to reduce the impact of any single investment on the overall portfolio. It involves spreading investments across different asset classes (e.g., stocks, bonds, real estate), sectors (e.g., technology, healthcare), and regions (e.g., domestic, international).

b. Benefits of Diversification:

Risk Reduction: Diversification helps mitigate the risk of significant losses associated with a single investment. When one asset performs poorly, others may perform well, offsetting losses and smoothing overall portfolio returns.

Potential for Enhanced Returns: Diversification allows investors to participate in different market segments that may outperform at different times. By capturing the performance of multiple assets, investors increase the potential for overall portfolio growth.

c. Diversification Strategies:

Asset Class Diversification: Allocate investments across different asset classes, such as stocks, bonds, real estate, commodities, and cash. Each asset class has its own risk and return characteristics, and diversifying across them reduces exposure to any single asset class's performance.

Sector Diversification: Invest in a broad range of sectors, such as technology, healthcare, consumer goods, and finance. This strategy helps spread risk across industries and reduces vulnerability to sector-specific events or economic changes.

Geographic Diversification: Allocate investments across different regions, including domestic and international markets. Geographic diversification reduces the impact of country-specific risks, economic conditions, and political events.

Asset Allocation:

a. Definition: Asset allocation is the process of determining the appropriate mix of asset classes within a portfolio based on an investor's financial goals, risk tolerance, and investment horizon.

b. Importance of Asset Allocation:

Risk Management: Asset allocation allows investors to balance risk by allocating investments across different asset classes. This helps align the portfolio with the investor's risk tolerance and reduces exposure to any single asset class's performance.

Return Potential: Asset allocation also aims to maximize returns based on the investor's risk profile. By investing in different asset classes that have varying risk-return characteristics, investors can potentially optimize their portfolio's return potential.

c. Strategies for Asset Allocation:

Strategic Asset Allocation: Establish a long-term target asset allocation based on the investor's risk tolerance and investment goals. Regularly rebalance the portfolio to maintain the desired allocation as market conditions and investment performance change.

Tactical Asset Allocation: Make short-term adjustments to the portfolio's asset allocation based on the investor's assessment of market conditions and economic outlook. This strategy involves actively managing the portfolio to exploit perceived opportunities or mitigate risks.

Considerations for Diversification and Asset Allocation:

a. Risk Tolerance: Assess your risk tolerance, which depends on your financial goals, time horizon, and ability to withstand market fluctuations. Diversification and asset allocation should align with your risk tolerance to ensure a comfortable investment experience.

b. Research and Analysis: Conduct thorough research and analysis of different asset classes, sectors, and regions. Consider historical performance, risk factors, correlation patterns, and future growth potential to make informed decisions about diversification and asset allocation.

c. Regular Monitoring and Rebalancing: Regularly review your portfolio's performance and adjust the asset allocation if needed. Rebalancing ensures that the portfolio remains aligned with your intended risk exposure and long-term objectives.

Diversification and asset allocation are essential components of a well-constructed investment portfolio. By spreading investments across different asset classes, sectors, and regions, investors can manage risk, potentially enhance returns, and achieve a balanced portfolio tailored to their risk tolerance and financial goals. Combining diligent research, regular monitoring, and periodic rebalancing, investors can build a strong investment foundation that withstands market fluctuations and supports long-term success. Remember, diversification does not guarantee profits or protect against losses, but it is an effective risk management strategy that can enhance the potential for achieving investment objectives.

Setting Stop-Loss Orders and Risk Management Techniques: Safeguarding Your Investments

Successful investing requires not only identifying profit opportunities but also managing and mitigating potential risks. Setting stop-loss orders and employing risk management techniques are vital strategies that help protect your investments from significant losses. In this chapter, we will discuss the concept of stop-loss orders, risk management techniques, and their role in preserving capital and maintaining disciplined investing.

Understanding Stop-Loss Orders:

a. Definition: A stop-loss order is a predefined instruction to sell a security when it reaches a specific price level. It serves as a risk management tool that helps limit potential losses by automatically triggering a sell order if the security's price falls below a predetermined threshold.

b. Benefits of Stop-Loss Orders:

Capital Preservation: Stop-loss orders provide an effective means of protecting capital by limiting potential losses on individual investments. They allow investors to exit a position before significant declines occur.

Emotional Discipline: Stop-loss orders help enforce disciplined investing by removing the emotional component from decision-making. They prevent investors from holding onto losing positions in the hope of a turnaround and help avoid impulsive or emotionally driven selling decisions.

c. Setting Stop-Loss Orders:

Determining Stop-Loss Levels: Analyze the security's price history, support levels, resistance levels, and market trends to establish an appropriate stop-loss level. Consider the risk-reward ratio, volatility, and your risk tolerance when setting the stop-loss order.

Trailing Stop-Loss Orders: Trailing stop-loss orders are dynamic and adjust based on the security's price movement. The stop-loss level is set as a percentage or dollar amount below the highest price reached since the order was placed, allowing for potential profit capture while protecting against downside risk.

Risk Management Techniques:

a. Position Sizing: Determine the appropriate allocation of capital for each investment based on its risk and potential return. Avoid overconcentration in a single investment and maintain a well-diversified portfolio.

b. Asset Allocation: Allocate investments across different asset classes, such as stocks, bonds, and real estate, to reduce exposure to any single asset's risk. Asset allocation helps spread risk and potentially enhance overall portfolio returns.

c. Hedging: Implement hedging strategies, such as using options or futures contracts, to protect against adverse market movements. Hedging can help mitigate potential losses and reduce portfolio volatility.

d. Portfolio Rebalancing: Regularly review and rebalance your portfolio to maintain the desired asset allocation. Rebalancing involves selling overperforming assets and buying underperforming assets, ensuring the portfolio remains aligned with your investment objectives and risk tolerance.

e. Diversification: Diversify your investments across different asset classes, sectors, and geographical regions to reduce concentration risk. A diversified portfolio can provide a buffer against specific market or industry risks.

Monitoring and Adjusting Risk Management Strategies:

a. Regular Portfolio Review: Conduct periodic portfolio reviews to assess the performance of individual investments, the overall portfolio, and the effectiveness of risk management strategies.

Stay informed about market trends and adjust your risk management techniques as needed.

b. Flexibility and Adaptability: Be prepared to adjust your risk management strategies based on changing market conditions, economic outlook, or individual investment performance. Flexibility and adaptability are essential for effectively managing risks.

c. Continuous Learning: Stay updated with industry news, economic indicators, and market trends. Continuously educate yourself about risk management techniques and refine your skills to improve your investment decision-making.

Setting stop-loss orders and employing risk management techniques are crucial for protecting your investments and maintaining disciplined investing. Stop-loss orders help limit losses and remove emotional biases, while risk management techniques like position sizing, asset allocation, hedging, and diversification provide a comprehensive approach to managing risk. Regular monitoring, adjustment of strategies, and continuous learning will further enhance your risk management capabilities. By incorporating these practices into your investment approach, you can safeguard your investments, mitigate potential losses, and improve your long-term investment outcomes.

Avoiding Common Investment Pitfalls: A Guide to Smarter Investing

Investing can be a rewarding endeavor, but it's important to navigate the financial markets with caution and avoid common pitfalls that can undermine your investment success. By being aware of these pitfalls and taking proactive steps to mitigate them, you can improve your chances of achieving your financial goals. In this area, we will discuss some common investment pitfalls and provide insights on how to avoid them.

Emotional Decision Making:

One of the most significant pitfalls investors face is making decisions based on emotions rather than sound judgment. I've lost thousands of dollars because I let my emotions get the best of me. Emotions such as fear, greed, and impatience can lead to poor investment choices. To avoid this pitfall, it is crucial to:

Maintain a long-term perspective: Focus on your investment goals and resist the temptation to react to short-term market fluctuations.

Conduct thorough research: Base your investment decisions on objective analysis and data rather than emotional reactions.

Stick to your investment plan: Develop a well-defined investment strategy and stick to it, avoiding impulsive buying or selling decisions driven by emotions.

Lack of Diversification:

Failing to diversify your investment portfolio is another common pitfall that exposes you to unnecessary risk. Concentrating your investments in a single stock, sector, or asset class can leave you vulnerable to significant losses if that particular investment performs poorly. To avoid this pitfall, consider:

Spreading your investments across different asset classes: Diversify your portfolio by investing in stocks, bonds, real estate, and other assets.

Allocating investments across sectors: Avoid overexposure to any one industry or sector by investing in a broad range of sectors.

Geographic diversification: Consider international investments to reduce the impact of country-specific risks.

Chasing Performance:

Chasing the latest investment fad or hot stock can lead to poor investment outcomes. Many investors fall into the trap of buying assets that have already experienced substantial gains, only to see them decline in value. To avoid this pitfall:

Focus on fundamentals: Instead of chasing short-term performance, assess the underlying fundamentals and long-term prospects of an investment.

Stick to your investment strategy: Avoid making impulsive changes to your portfolio based on short-term market trends or performance.

Ignoring Risk Management:

Failing to implement risk management strategies can expose your investments to unnecessary risks. To avoid this pitfall, consider the following:

Setting stop-loss orders: Use stop-loss orders to automatically sell a security if it reaches a predetermined price, limiting potential losses.

Regular portfolio review: Monitor your portfolio regularly to identify underperforming investments and make adjustments as needed.

Adequate diversification: Diversify your portfolio to spread risk and reduce exposure to any single investment.

Overlooking Costs and Fees:

High investment costs and fees can eat into your returns over time. To avoid this pitfall:

Compare investment costs: Research and compare fees associated with different investment products and platforms.

Consider low-cost options: Look for low-cost index funds, ETFs, or brokerage accounts with competitive fees.

Lack of Patience and Discipline:

Investing is a long-term endeavor that requires patience and discipline. Trying to time the market or making frequent changes to your portfolio can undermine your investment success. To avoid this pitfall:

Maintain a long-term perspective: Remember that investing is a marathon, not a sprint. Stay focused on your long-term financial goals.

Stick to your investment plan: Develop a well-thought-out investment strategy and resist the urge to make frequent changes based on short-term market movements.

Avoiding common investment pitfalls is crucial for long-term investment success. By staying disciplined, diversifying your portfolio, conducting thorough research, and managing risks, you can navigate the financial markets more effectively. Remember, investing is a journey that requires continuous learning and adaptation. By avoiding these pitfalls, you can enhance your investment outcomes and work towards achieving your financial objectives.

CHAPTER NINE

Retirement Planning and Beyond: Securing Your Financial Future

Retirement planning is a critical aspect of financial management that ensures a secure and comfortable future. However, retirement is not the end of financial responsibilities but rather a new phase that requires ongoing management and decision-making. Now, let's explore retirement planning strategies and considerations, as well as important financial considerations beyond retirement.

Retirement Planning:

a. Define Your Retirement Goals:

Assess your desired lifestyle: Determine the lifestyle you want to maintain during retirement, considering factors such as housing, healthcare, travel, and hobbies.

Estimate retirement expenses: Evaluate your current spending patterns and adjust for anticipated changes in retirement, such as reduced work-related costs and potential healthcare expenses.

b. Calculate Retirement Savings Needs:

Evaluate your retirement income sources: Assess income from pensions, Social Security, and other retirement accounts.

Determine the savings gap: Calculate the amount you need to save to meet your retirement goals, considering inflation, investment returns, and the length of your retirement.

c. Develop a Retirement Savings Strategy:

Start early: Take advantage of the power of compounding by beginning to save for retirement as early as possible.

Maximize retirement account contributions: Contribute to tax-advantaged retirement accounts like 401(k)s or IRAs and take advantage of any employer matching contributions.

Diversify investments: Allocate your retirement savings across a mix of asset classes to balance risk and potential returns.

Monitor and adjust: Regularly review your retirement savings plan and make necessary adjustments based on changing circumstances.

Managing Retirement Income:

a. Develop a Withdrawal Strategy:

Determine a sustainable withdrawal rate: Establish a withdrawal rate that balances income needs with the longevity of your retirement savings.

Consider tax implications: Be mindful of the tax consequences of different withdrawal strategies, such as managing taxable and tax-advantaged account distributions.

b. Maintain an Emergency Fund:

Preserve liquidity: Set aside funds in a liquid and easily accessible account to cover unexpected expenses or emergencies during retirement.

c. Consider Long-Term Care:

Evaluate long-term care insurance: Assess the need for long-term care insurance to protect against the potentially high costs of medical and personal care services in later years.

Estate Planning:

a. Create or Update Your Estate Plan:

Draft a will: Clearly outline how your assets should be distributed after your passing.

Establish a power of attorney: Designate someone to make financial and medical decisions on your behalf in case of incapacitation.

Consider trusts: Explore the benefits of trusts to protect assets, minimize taxes, and manage the transfer of wealth.

b. Review Beneficiary Designations:

Ensure your retirement accounts and insurance policies have

updated beneficiary designations to align with your estate planning goals.

Philanthropy and Legacy:

a. Charitable Giving:

Explore philanthropic endeavors: Consider incorporating charitable giving into your retirement and estate planning to support causes that are important to you.

b. Intergenerational Wealth Transfer:

Develop a plan for passing on wealth to future generations, considering tax implications and the values you wish to instill in your heirs.

Retirement planning is not a one-time event but an ongoing process that requires regular monitoring and adjustment. By diligently saving, developing a withdrawal strategy, and considering estate planning and philanthropic goals, you can secure your financial future and leave a lasting legacy.

Creating a Retirement Savings Plan: Building a Financial Foundation for Retirement

Planning for retirement is a crucial step in ensuring financial security and independence during your golden years. Creating a retirement savings plan provides a roadmap to accumulate the necessary funds to support your desired lifestyle after you stop working. In this chapter, we will outline the key steps involved in creating an effective retirement savings plan.

Assess Your Current Financial Situation:

a. Determine Your Retirement Goals:

Define your desired retirement age: Consider when you want to retire and how many years you anticipate living in retirement.

Estimate your retirement expenses: Evaluate your current spending habits and project future expenses, accounting for inflation, healthcare costs, and other factors.

Consider lifestyle choices: Determine the kind of retirement lifestyle you envision, including travel, hobbies, and potential housing changes.

b. Evaluate Your Existing Retirement Savings:

Review retirement accounts: Take stock of your current retirement savings, including employer-sponsored plans (e.g., 401(k), 403(b)) and individual retirement accounts (IRAs).

Assess Social Security benefits: Estimate your expected Social Security benefits based on your work history and projected retirement age.

Factor in other income sources: Consider any additional income sources, such as pensions or rental properties, which may contribute to your retirement funds.

Calculate Your Retirement Savings Target:

a. Determine Your Retirement Income Needs:

Evaluate retirement expenses: Analyze your estimated retirement expenses, considering both essential costs (e.g., housing, healthcare) and discretionary spending.

Consider income replacement ratio: Aim to replace a certain percentage of your pre-retirement income (e.g., 70-80%) to maintain your standard of living.

b. Calculate Your Retirement Savings Gap:

Assess your retirement savings shortfall: Subtract your expected retirement income from your retirement income needs to determine the gap that needs to be filled through savings and investments.

Utilize retirement calculators: Take advantage of online tools and retirement calculators to estimate the savings needed to meet your retirement goals.

Develop a Retirement Savings Strategy:

a. Set Clear Savings Goals:

Determine how much to save: Establish a savings target based on your retirement income needs and desired timeline.

Break it down: Break down your savings target into annual or monthly contributions to make it more manageable.

b. Maximize Employer-Sponsored Plans:

Take advantage of employer matches: Contribute enough to your employer-sponsored retirement plan to maximize any matching contributions offered by your employer.

Understand plan features: Familiarize yourself with the features and investment options available in your workplace retirement plan.

c. Explore Individual Retirement Accounts (IRAs):

Consider Traditional and Roth IRAs: Evaluate the tax advantages and eligibility criteria for Traditional and Roth IRAs to determine which is most suitable for your situation.

Contribute regularly: Contribute to your IRA consistently, either through regular contributions or automated transfers.

d. Invest for Growth:

Determine an appropriate asset allocation: Strike a balance between risk and reward by allocating your retirement savings across different asset classes (e.g., stocks, bonds).

Review and adjust periodically: Monitor your investments regularly and make adjustments as needed to stay aligned with your retirement goals and risk tolerance.

Monitor and Adjust Your Plan:

a. Regularly Review Your Progress:

Assess your savings growth: Track the growth of your retirement savings and compare it against your targeted savings goals.

Review your investment performance: Evaluate the performance of your investments and consider rebalancing your portfolio if necessary.

b. Make Adjustments as Needed:

Increase savings contributions: If possible, boost your savings contributions as your income grows or whenever you have the opportunity.

Adjust your investment strategy: Reevaluate your asset allocation and risk tolerance periodically, making changes as needed to align with your retirement timeline and goals.

Seek professional advice: Consult with a financial advisor who specializes in retirement planning to get personalized guidance and ensure you are on track.

Creating a retirement savings plan is a crucial step in securing your financial future. By assessing your current situation, setting clear savings goals, maximizing retirement accounts, and regularly monitoring your progress, you can build a solid foundation for a comfortable retirement. Remember to adapt your plan as circumstances change and seek professional guidance when needed to optimize your retirement savings strategy.

Maximizing Retirement Account Contributions: Supercharging Your Savings for Retirement

Retirement accounts, such as 401(k)s, IRAs, and other tax-advantaged plans, offer individuals an opportunity to save and grow their wealth for retirement while enjoying potential tax benefits. Maximizing contributions to these accounts is a powerful way to accelerate your retirement savings. In this chapter, we will explore strategies and considerations for maximizing your retirement account contributions.

Understand Contribution Limits and Eligibility:

a. 401(k) Contributions:

Know the annual limits: Stay informed about the maximum contribution limit set by the IRS for 401(k) plans each year.

Employer matching contributions: Take advantage of any matching contributions offered by your employer, as it is essentially free money added to your retirement savings.

Consider catch-up contributions: If you are age 50 or older, take advantage of catch-up contributions that allow you to contribute additional funds beyond the regular limit.

b. Individual Retirement Accounts (IRAs):

Traditional IRA vs. Roth IRA: Understand the contribution limits and tax implications of each type of IRA.

Assess your eligibility: Ensure you meet the income requirements for making contributions to a Roth IRA and deducting contributions to a Traditional IRA.

Develop a Contribution Strategy:

a. Set Clear Savings Goals:

Determine your desired retirement income: Calculate your estimated retirement income needs and use that as a guide to set savings goals.

Break it down: Divide your savings goal into manageable annual or monthly contribution targets.

b. Prioritize Retirement Contributions:

Make it a priority: Allocate a significant portion of your income towards retirement contributions, treating them as essential expenses rather than discretionary spending.

Automate contributions: Set up automatic contributions from your paycheck or bank account to ensure consistent and disciplined saving.

c. Coordinate Contributions with Employer Plans:

Contribute enough to maximize employer match: Aim to contribute at least enough to receive the full matching contribution from your employer, as it represents an immediate return on your investment.

Explore additional retirement savings options: If you have maxed out your employer-sponsored retirement plan contributions, consider opening an IRA to further boost your retirement savings.

Leverage Catch-up Contributions:

a. 401(k) Catch-up Contributions:

Understand the rules: If you are age 50 or older, familiarize yourself with the catch-up contribution limits and rules specific to 401(k) plans.

Take advantage of the opportunity: Make the most of the catch-up contribution allowance to accelerate your savings in the years leading up to retirement.

b. IRA Catch-up Contributions:

Consider Traditional and Roth IRA catch-up contributions: If you are 50 or older, take advantage of the additional contribution limits for IRAs to boost your retirement savings.

Consider Tax Optimization Strategies:

a. Traditional 401(k) Contributions:

Tax-deferred growth: Contribute to a Traditional 401(k) to reduce your taxable income in the current year and allow your investments to grow tax-deferred until retirement.

b. Roth Contributions:

Tax-free withdrawals: Consider contributing to a Roth 401(k) or Roth IRA if you expect your tax rate to be higher in retirement, as qualified withdrawals are tax-free.

Maximizing your retirement account contributions is a smart and effective way to supercharge your savings for retirement. By understanding contribution limits, developing a contribution strategy, leveraging catch-up contributions, considering tax optimization strategies, and seeking professional guidance, you can make the most of your retirement accounts and significantly enhance your financial security in retirement. Start early, be consistent, and prioritize your retirement savings to create a solid foundation for a comfortable and enjoyable retirement.

Social Security and Medicare Considerations: Navigating Government Programs for Retirement

Social Security and Medicare are two vital government programs that play a significant role in retirement planning. Understanding how these programs work and the factors that impact your benefits is crucial for making informed decisions. Let's talk about the key considerations related to Social Security and Medicare to help you maximize your benefits and ensure comprehensive healthcare coverage during retirement.

Social Security:

a. Understanding Social Security Benefits:

Eligibility requirements: Familiarize yourself with the eligibility criteria, which are based on your work history and the number of credits earned.

Benefit calculations: Learn how your Social Security benefits are calculated based on your earnings history and the age at which you choose to start receiving benefits.

Full retirement age: Determine your full retirement age (FRA), which is the age at which you can receive full Social Security retirement benefits.

b. Considerations for Claiming Social Security Benefits:

Early vs. delayed claiming: Evaluate the advantages and disadvantages of claiming benefits early (reduced monthly payments) or delaying them (increased monthly payments).

Spousal benefits: Understand the spousal benefit options available, such as claiming based on your own earnings or claiming a spousal benefit based on your spouse's earnings.

c. Maximizing Social Security Benefits:

Earnings optimization: Strategize your earnings leading up to retirement to maximize your average indexed monthly earnings (AIME), which is a factor in benefit calculations.

Coordination with other retirement income: Consider how your Social Security benefits will align with other sources of retirement income, such as pensions or investment accounts.

Medicare:

a. Medicare Basics:

Enrollment periods: Understand the initial enrollment period, general enrollment period, and special enrollment periods to ensure timely enrollment without penalties.

Medicare coverage components: Familiarize yourself with the different parts of Medicare, including Part A (hospital insurance), Part B (medical insurance), Part C (Medicare Advantage), and Part D (prescription drug coverage).

b. Medicare Coverage Options:

Original Medicare vs. Medicare Advantage: Compare the advantages and limitations of Original Medicare, which includes Parts A and B, with Medicare Advantage plans offered by private insurance companies.

Supplemental coverage: Explore Medicare Supplement Insurance (Medigap) policies that can help cover out-of-pocket expenses not covered by Original Medicare.

c. Cost Considerations:

Premiums, deductibles, and co-payments: Understand the costs associated with Medicare coverage and how they may impact your budget.

Income-related monthly adjustment amount (IRMAA): Be aware of the additional premium amounts charged to higher-income individuals.

d. Prescription Drug Coverage:

Part D coverage: Evaluate the importance of prescription drug coverage and consider enrolling in a Part D plan to help manage medication costs.

Formularies and coverage tiers: Understand how drug formularies and coverage tiers can affect out-of-pocket expenses for medications.

Planning Strategies:

a. Coordinate Social Security and Medicare:

Timing considerations: Determine the optimal age to claim Social Security benefits while considering Medicare eligibility and potential penalties for late enrollment.

Health coverage during the waiting period: If retiring before Medicare eligibility, explore options such as COBRA or individual health insurance plans to bridge the gap.

b. Seek Professional Guidance:

Consult a financial advisor or retirement specialist: Seek advice from professionals well-versed in Social Security and Medicare to navigate complex rules, optimize benefits, and ensure appropriate healthcare coverage.

Social Security and Medicare are critical components of retirement planning, providing financial support and healthcare coverage during your golden years. By understanding the intricacies of these programs, making informed decisions regarding benefit-claiming strategies, and coordinating Social Security and Medicare enrollment, you can optimize your retirement income and ensure comprehensive healthcare coverage.

Legacy Planning and Estate Management: Securing Your Wealth for Future Generations

Legacy planning and estate management are essential components of comprehensive financial planning. They involve creating a strategy to preserve and distribute your wealth, assets, and values to future generations. In this section, we will discuss the key considerations and strategies for effective legacy planning and estate management.

Understanding Legacy Planning:

a. Defining your legacy: Reflect on the values, beliefs, and goals you wish to pass on to future generations. Consider the impact you want to have on your family, community, or charitable causes.

b. Identifying your objectives:

Asset distribution: Determine how you want your assets to be distributed among your heirs, beneficiaries, and charitable organizations.

Minimizing taxes: Explore strategies to minimize estate taxes, gift taxes, and other potential tax liabilities.

Protecting assets: Consider strategies to protect your assets from potential risks, such as lawsuits or creditors.

Estate Planning:

a. Creating a comprehensive estate plan:

Will: Draft a legally binding document that outlines how your assets should be distributed upon your death and appoints an executor to manage the process.

Trusts: Explore the benefits of various types of trusts, such as revocable living trusts, irrevocable trusts, and charitable trusts, to manage and distribute assets according to your wishes while minimizing taxes and maintaining privacy.

Power of attorney and healthcare directives: Designate individuals to make financial and medical decisions on your behalf in the event of incapacity.

Beneficiary designations: Review and update beneficiary

designations on financial accounts, retirement plans, and life insurance policies to ensure they align with your wishes.

b. Engaging professional assistance:

Estate planning attorney: Consult an experienced estate planning attorney to help create and review your estate plan, ensuring it is legally sound and aligned with your objectives.

Financial advisor: Collaborate with a financial advisor who can provide guidance on tax-efficient strategies, asset allocation, and wealth transfer considerations.

Charitable Giving and Philanthropy:

a. Charitable objectives:

Determine your philanthropic goals: Identify causes or organizations that align with your values and create a meaningful impact.

Establish charitable giving strategies: Explore options such as creating a donor-advised fund, setting up a private foundation, or incorporating charitable bequests in your estate plan.

Regular Review and Updates:

a. Periodic estate plan reviews:

Tax law changes: Stay informed about changes in tax laws that may impact estate planning strategies and consider necessary adjustments.

Beneficiary updates: Ensure that beneficiary designations and asset titling align with your current wishes.

Communicating Your Plan:

a. Open dialogue with family members:

Discuss your intentions: Communicate your estate plan and legacy goals with your loved ones to manage expectations and reduce potential conflicts.

Share important information: Provide family members with relevant details, such as the location of important documents, contact information for professionals, and your wishes regarding end-of-life decisions.

Seeking Professional Guidance:

a. Estate planning attorney: Engage the services of an experienced estate planning attorney to ensure your estate plan is legally sound and reflects your objectives.

b. Financial advisor: Collaborate with a financial advisor who specializes in estate planning to integrate your legacy planning goals with your overall financial strategy.

Legacy planning and estate management allow you to leave a lasting impact on future generations and ensure the smooth transfer of your assets while minimizing tax burdens. By understanding the key components of legacy planning, engaging professional assistance, regularly reviewing your estate plan, and fostering open communication with your loved ones, you can establish a solid framework for preserving your wealth and values for years to come.

CHAPTER TEN

Adapting Investment Strategies to Different Economic Cycles: Capitalizing on Opportunities Across Market Phases

The performance of investment strategies can vary significantly depending on the stage of the economic cycle. To maximize returns and manage risks effectively, it is crucial to adapt your investment approach based on the prevailing economic conditions. In this chapter, we will explore strategies for adjusting your investment strategies to different economic cycles.

Understanding Economic Cycles:

a. Expansion phase:

Characteristics: Increased consumer spending, rising business profits, low unemployment, and favorable credit conditions.

Investment strategies: Allocate a higher percentage of your

portfolio to growth-oriented assets, such as stocks, to capitalize on upward trends in the market.

b. Peak phase:

Characteristics: Slowing economic growth, tightening credit conditions, and potential signs of excesses or imbalances in the economy.

Investment strategies: Consider gradually reducing exposure to riskier assets and shifting toward defensive investments, such as bonds and dividend-paying stocks.

c. Contraction phase:

Characteristics: Economic decline, rising unemployment, reduced consumer spending, and declining corporate profits.

Investment strategies: Focus on preserving capital and minimizing losses by emphasizing fixed-income investments, cash equivalents, and defensive sectors.

d. Trough phase:

Characteristics: The economy reaches its lowest point, but signs of recovery may emerge, such as increased business activity and improved investor sentiment.

Investment strategies: Gradually increase exposure to cyclical assets, such as stocks, as the economy shows signs of stabilization and potential for growth.

Sector Rotation:

a. Cyclical sectors: During expansion phases, sectors such as technology, consumer discretionary, and industrials tend to perform well. Allocate a portion of your portfolio to these sectors during favorable economic conditions.

b. Defensive sectors: In contraction or recessionary phases, defensive sectors like utilities, healthcare, and consumer staples tend to provide more stability and downside protection. Consider increasing exposure to these sectors during economic downturns.

Asset Allocation Adjustments:

a. Equities: Increase exposure to equities during expansion phases when stocks tend to outperform. Consider diversifying across various market capitalizations and regions to manage risks.

b. Fixed-income: Increase allocations to high-quality bonds and fixed-income instruments during contraction phases to mitigate volatility and generate income.

c. Cash: Holding cash equivalents can provide liquidity and flexibility to take advantage of investment opportunities during uncertain or volatile market conditions.

Active vs. Passive Strategies:

a. Active management: During periods of market volatility or economic transitions, active management strategies that focus on stock selection and tactical asset allocation can help navigate changing market dynamics.

b. Passive management: In more stable economic conditions,

passive investment strategies, such as index funds or ETFs, can offer cost-effective exposure to broad market trends.

Long-Term Focus:

a. Avoid short-term market timing: Attempting to time the market consistently is challenging. Focus on long-term investment goals and avoid making impulsive decisions based on short-term economic fluctuations.

b. Dollar-cost averaging: Regularly invest a fixed amount over time, regardless of market conditions, to reduce the impact of market volatility and take advantage of potential opportunities at different economic stages.

Adapting investment strategies to different economic cycles is essential for optimizing returns and managing risks effectively. By understanding the characteristics of each economic phase, adjusting sector allocations, optimizing asset allocation, considering active vs. passive strategies, practicing risk management, and maintaining a long-term focus, you can position yourself to capitalize on opportunities and navigate the complexities of the economic cycle. Remember, flexibility, informed decision-making, and periodic portfolio reviews are key to adapting to changing economic conditions and achieving your investment objectives.

The Impact of Geopolitical Events on Investments: Navigating Uncertainty in Global Markets

Geopolitical events, such as political conflicts, trade disputes, regulatory changes, and economic sanctions, have a significant impact on financial markets and can create both risks and opportunities for investors. Understanding how these events shape market dynamics is crucial for making informed investment decisions. In this section, we will talk about the impact of geopolitical events on investments and discuss strategies for navigating the resulting uncertainty.

Market Volatility and Investor Sentiment:

Geopolitical events often trigger increased market volatility as investors react to unexpected developments. Heightened uncertainty and fear can lead to sharp price fluctuations, affecting various asset classes. Investor sentiment plays a crucial role during such periods, as market participants may become more risk-averse or seek safe-haven assets.

Sector and Industry-Specific Impact:

Different geopolitical events can have varying effects on specific sectors and industries. For instance:

a. Trade disputes: Tariffs or trade restrictions can impact industries dependent on global supply chains, such as manufacturing and technology.

b. Political instability: Events like elections or regime changes can influence sectors such as energy, infrastructure, and financial services, depending on the policies of new governments.

c. Regulatory changes: Alterations in regulations can impact specific sectors, such as healthcare, banking, or technology, leading to shifts in investor sentiment and market performance.

Regional and Global Market Reactions:

Geopolitical events often have a more pronounced impact on specific regions or countries. For example:

a. Regional conflicts: Political tensions and conflicts in specific regions can disrupt economies, affect currency values, and create localized market turbulence.

b. Global economic impact: Large-scale geopolitical events, such as trade wars or global financial crises, can have far-reaching consequences, impacting global markets and creating systemic risks.

Opportunities in Market Disruptions:

Geopolitical events can also present investment opportunities:

a. Safe-haven assets: During periods of uncertainty, investors may seek refuge in traditional safe-haven assets like gold, government bonds, or stable currencies.

b. Sector rotation: Changes in political or regulatory landscapes can create opportunities for sector rotation, as new policies may favor specific industries or impact market leaders.

c. Emerging markets: Geopolitical events can create buying opportunities in emerging markets if investors believe that short-term disruptions will not hinder long-term growth prospects.

Risk Management Strategies:

a. Diversification: Maintaining a diversified portfolio across asset classes, sectors, and regions helps mitigate the impact of geopolitical events on individual investments.

b. Hedging: Utilizing hedging strategies, such as options or futures contracts, can protect against potential downside risks in volatile markets.

c. Active monitoring: Stay informed about geopolitical events through reputable news sources, research reports, and market analysis. Continuously assess the potential impact on your investments and make adjustments as needed.

Long-Term Perspective:

While geopolitical events can create short-term market disruptions, it is essential to maintain a long-term perspective when investing. Economic fundamentals and long-term trends often prevail over short-term volatility caused by geopolitical events. Avoid making impulsive decisions based solely on the latest headlines.

Geopolitical events have a significant impact on investments, shaping market volatility, sector performance, and investor sentiment. By staying informed, diversifying portfolios, implementing risk management strategies, maintaining a long-term perspective, and seeking professional guidance, investors can navigate the uncertainties presented by geopolitical events. Remember, patience and a disciplined approach are key when managing investments in the face of geopolitical challenges.

CHAPTER 11

Resources and Tools for Investors: Empowering Financial Success

Financial Education and Information:

a. Online Platforms and Blogs: Utilize reputable financial websites, blogs, and forums that offer educational content, investment insights, and market analysis. Examples include Investopedia, The Motley Fool, and Seeking Alpha.

b. Webinars and Podcasts: Engage with webinars and podcasts hosted by financial experts and industry professionals. These platforms provide valuable information on investing, personal finance, retirement planning, and other relevant topics.

c. Financial Literacy Courses: Consider enrolling in financial literacy courses offered by educational institutions, community centers, or online platforms. These courses cover a wide range of topics, including investment fundamentals, risk management, and retirement planning.

Investment Research Tools:

a. Online Brokerage Platforms: Choose a reputable online brokerage platform that offers comprehensive research tools and resources. Look for platforms that provide access to company financials, analyst reports, market data, and real-time news.

b. Stock Screeners: Use stock screeners to filter and identify investment opportunities based on specific criteria such as market capitalization, industry sector, or financial metrics. Popular stock screeners include Finviz and Yahoo Finance.

c. Investment Newsletters: Subscribe to investment newsletters that provide in-depth analysis, stock recommendations, and market insights from experienced analysts. These newsletters can help you stay informed about market trends and potential investment opportunities.

Retirement Planning Tools:

a. Retirement Calculators: Take advantage of retirement calculators available online to estimate your retirement needs, determine savings goals, and evaluate the impact of different investment strategies. Tools like Vanguard's Retirement Nest Egg Calculator and Fidelity's Retirement Score can be helpful.

b. Retirement Planning Guides: Access retirement planning guides that provide step-by-step instructions and actionable advice on various aspects of retirement planning, including asset allocation, Social Security optimization, and withdrawal strategies.

Financial Apps and Budgeting Tools:

a. Budgeting Apps: Use budgeting apps like Mint, Personal Capital, or You Need a Budget (YNAB) to track expenses, set financial goals, and manage cash flow. These apps provide insights into spending patterns and help you make informed decisions about saving and investing.

b. Portfolio Tracking Apps: Consider portfolio tracking apps such as Morningstar, SigFig, or Betterment that allow you to monitor your investment performance, asset allocation, and diversification across multiple accounts.

Financial Advisors and Professionals:

a. Certified Financial Planners (CFPs): Engage with certified financial planners who can provide personalized advice on investment strategies, retirement planning, and wealth management. Look for CFPs with expertise in serving Generation X clients.

b. Robo-Advisors: Consider robo-advisory services like Wealthfront, Betterment, or Vanguard Personal Advisor Services that provide algorithm-based investment management with low fees. These platforms offer tailored investment portfolios based on your risk tolerance and financial goals.

As we navigate our financial journeys, leveraging the right resources and tools is crucial for making informed investment decisions and achieving long-term financial success. By tapping into financial education platforms, utilizing investment research tools, accessing retirement planning resources, leveraging financial apps, and seeking guidance from professionals, investors can empower themselves to navigate the complexities of the investment landscape and build a secure financial future. Remember, knowledge and proactive engagement are key to unlocking the full potential of your investments.

Online Platforms and Investment Apps: Empowering Investors in the Digital Age

The rise of technology has revolutionized the investment landscape, providing investors with convenient access to a wide range of online platforms and investment apps. These platforms and apps offer a multitude of tools and resources that empower individuals to manage their investments efficiently, make informed decisions, and stay updated on market trends. Let's discuss the benefits and features of online platforms and investment apps, highlighting their role in shaping the investment experience.

Online Brokerage Platforms:

Online brokerage platforms have democratized investing, allowing individuals to trade stocks, bonds, mutual funds, and other securities with ease. These platforms offer a host of features, including:

a. Account Management: Investors can create and manage their investment accounts online, with the ability to view portfolio holdings, transaction history, and performance metrics in real-time.

b. Research Tools: Online brokerages provide access to research reports, market data, analyst ratings, and financial news, helping investors make informed decisions.

c. Trading Capabilities: Investors can place trades, set limit orders, and monitor market activity directly through the platform, providing convenience and control over their investment transactions.

d. Education and Insights: Many online brokerages offer educational resources, webinars, and market insights to help investors enhance their knowledge and make better-informed investment decisions.

Robo-Advisory Platforms:

Robo-advisory platforms combine technology and algorithms to provide automated investment management services. These platforms offer the following benefits:

a. Automated Portfolio Management: Robo-advisors use algorithms to construct and manage diversified investment portfolios based on an investor's risk tolerance, financial goals, and time horizon.

b. Low Costs: Robo-advisors typically have lower fees compared to traditional investment advisors, making them an attractive option for cost-conscious investors.

c. Goal-Based Investing: Investors can set specific financial goals, such as retirement or education funding, and the robo-advisor will customize the investment strategy accordingly.

d. Rebalancing and Tax Optimization: Robo-advisors automatically rebalance portfolios and employ tax-loss harvesting strategies to minimize tax liabilities and maintain portfolio efficiency.

Financial Aggregators:

Financial aggregators bring together information from various financial accounts into a single platform, providing a comprehensive overview of an individual's financial position. Key features include:

a. Account Aggregation: Users can link their bank accounts, investment accounts, credit cards, and other financial accounts to aggregate and track their overall net worth and cash flow.

b. Expense Tracking: Financial aggregators categorize and analyze spending patterns, providing insights into budgeting and expense management.

c. Goal Tracking: Users can set financial goals, such as saving for a down payment or paying off debt, and track their progress towards achieving those goals.

d. Financial Planning Tools: Some aggregators offer financial planning tools that help users create budgets, plan for retirement, and simulate different scenarios to assess their financial future.

Investment Apps:

Investment apps have gained popularity for their user-friendly interfaces and accessibility. These apps offer the following features:

a. Easy Account Setup: Investment apps simplify the account setup process, allowing investors to open brokerage accounts or retirement accounts quickly and easily.

b. Fractional Share Investing: Some apps enable users to invest in fractional shares, making it affordable to buy shares of expensive stocks and diversify their portfolios with smaller amounts of capital.

c. Automated Investing: Investment apps offer automated investment features where users can set recurring investments, round-up spare change from transactions, or opt for pre-selected portfolios.

d. Social Trading and Education: Certain apps provide social trading functionalities, allowing users to follow and learn from successful investors, share insights, and participate in investment communities.

Online platforms and investment apps have transformed the investment landscape, giving investors unprecedented access to tools, research, and financial services. Whether through online brokerage platforms, robo-advisors, financial aggregators, or investment apps, individuals can now take control of their investments, make informed decisions, and manage their portfolios with ease. As technology continues to evolve, these platforms and apps will play an increasingly important role in empowering investors to achieve their financial goals and navigate the complexities of the investment world.

Financial Advisors and Robo-Advisors: Guiding Your Investment Journey

When it comes to managing investments, individuals have the option to seek guidance from financial advisors or leverage the services of robo-advisors. These two approaches offer distinct advantages and cater to different investor preferences and needs.

Financial Advisors:

Financial advisors are professionals who provide personalized investment advice and comprehensive financial planning services. Here are some key aspects of working with a financial advisor:

a. Expertise and Guidance: Financial advisors bring in-depth knowledge and experience to help investors develop tailored investment strategies aligned with their goals, risk tolerance, and time horizon.

b. Holistic Financial Planning: Advisors go beyond investment management, offering guidance on retirement planning, tax optimization, estate planning, insurance needs, and other aspects of an individual's financial life.

c. Personalized Approach: Advisors work closely with clients, considering their unique circumstances and goals to create customized investment portfolios and financial plans.

d. Behavioral Coaching: Advisors provide emotional support and behavioral coaching to help clients navigate market volatility, avoid common investment mistakes, and stay focused on long-term goals.

e. Regular Portfolio Reviews: Advisors conduct periodic portfolio reviews, assessing performance, rebalancing allocations, and making adjustments as needed to keep investments aligned with the client's objectives.

Robo-Advisors:

Robo-advisors are digital platforms that use algorithms and automation to provide investment management services. Here's what you need to know about robo-advisors:

a. Cost-Effective Solution: Robo-advisors often charge lower fees compared to traditional financial advisors, making them an attractive option for cost-conscious investors.

b. Automated Portfolio Construction: Robo-advisors use algorithms to construct diversified portfolios based on an investor's risk tolerance, financial goals, and time horizon. They employ modern portfolio theory principles to optimize asset allocation.

c. Easy Account Setup and Accessibility: Opening an account with a robo-advisor is typically quick and straightforward, and investors can access their portfolios and manage their investments through user-friendly mobile apps or online platforms.

d. Tax Efficiency: Robo-advisors employ tax-loss harvesting techniques to minimize tax liabilities. They automatically rebalance portfolios and strategically sell investments to offset capital gains with capital losses.

e. Limited Human Interaction: While robo-advisors offer digital support and access to customer service, they lack the personalized human touch that comes with working directly with a financial advisor.

Considerations and Choosing the Right Option:

a. Complexity of Financial Situation: If you have complex financial needs, intricate tax planning requirements, or specialized investment considerations, a financial advisor's personalized guidance may be more suitable.

b. Cost and Affordability: Consider your budget and the fees associated with each option. Financial advisors generally have higher fees, while robo-advisors offer cost-effective alternatives.

c. Communication Preferences: Evaluate how much importance you place on human interaction. Financial advisors provide a personal connection, while robo-advisors are more self-directed and automated.

d. Comfort with Technology: Robo-advisors heavily rely on technology and digital platforms. If you are comfortable with online interfaces and automated processes, a robo-advisor may be a good fit.

e. Level of Control: Financial advisors offer more flexibility and customization, allowing you to actively participate in the decision-making process. Robo-advisors, on the other hand, automate investment management with limited input from the investor.

Both financial advisors and robo-advisors have their advantages and serve different investor preferences. Financial advisors bring expertise, personalized guidance, and comprehensive financial planning, while robo-advisors offer cost-effectiveness, automation, and accessibility. Ultimately, the choice depends on your financial situation, goals, preferences, and the level of guidance and control you desire. Consider evaluating your needs and conducting thorough research to make an informed decision that aligns with your investment journey.

Investment Education and Courses: Building Knowledge for Financial Success

Investing can be complex and intimidating, especially for those who are new to the world of finance. Fortunately, there are numerous investment education resources and courses available to help individuals build their knowledge and confidence in managing their finances. In this chapter, we will explore the importance of investment education and the benefits of enrolling in investment courses to enhance your understanding and make informed investment decisions.

Importance of Investment Education:

a. Empowering Investors: Investment education empowers individuals to take control of their financial future by providing them with the knowledge and tools to make informed investment decisions.

b. Risk Management: Education helps investors understand the risks associated with different investment options, enabling them to mitigate potential losses and protect their capital.

c. Long-Term Perspective: Education teaches investors the importance of a long-term perspective, helping them resist the temptation of short-term market fluctuations and make decisions that align with their goals.

d. Expanding Investment Options: With education, investors gain a broader understanding of various investment avenues beyond traditional stocks and bonds, such as real estate, commodities, and alternative investments.

Types of Investment Education Resources:

a. Online Courses and Webinars: Online platforms offer a wide range of investment courses and webinars, allowing individuals to learn at their own pace and access expert knowledge from renowned professionals.

b. Books and Publications: Investment books written by industry experts provide in-depth knowledge and insights into investment strategies, market analysis, and personal finance. Financial publications and magazines also offer valuable information on market trends and investment opportunities.

c. Blogs and Podcasts: There are numerous investment-focused blogs and podcasts available, where industry experts and experienced investors share their insights, strategies, and tips.

d. Financial News and Websites: Staying updated with financial news and visiting reputable financial websites can provide investors with valuable information on market trends, analysis, and economic indicators.

Benefits of Investment Courses:

a. Structured Learning: Investment courses offer structured curricula and learning materials, providing a step-by-step approach to understanding investment concepts and strategies.

b. Expert Guidance: Courses often feature instructors with significant industry experience who can guide and answer questions, ensuring a thorough understanding of investment principles.

c. Interactive Learning: Many investment courses include interactive components, such as case studies, simulations, and group discussions, allowing participants to apply their knowledge and learn from real-world scenarios.

d. Networking Opportunities: Investment courses bring together individuals with similar interests, providing opportunities to network and learn from peers, mentors, and industry professionals.

e. Certification and Credibility: Completing reputable investment courses and earning certifications can enhance your credibility as an investor and may be beneficial for career advancement in finance-related fields.

Considerations for Choosing Investment Courses:

a. Relevance to Your Goals: Look for courses that align with your specific investment goals, whether it's stock market investing, real estate, retirement planning, or portfolio management.

b. Instructor Expertise: Research the credentials and experience of the course instructors to ensure they have the necessary knowledge and expertise to provide valuable insights.

c. Course Reviews and Reputation: Read reviews and seek recommendations from trusted sources to gauge the reputation and quality of the course before enrolling.

d. Flexibility and Accessibility: Consider your schedule and learning preferences. Look for courses that offer flexibility in terms of timing, format (online or in-person), and accessibility to accommodate your needs.

Investment education is a crucial foundation for making informed investment decisions and achieving financial success. By taking advantage of investment education resources and enrolling in relevant courses, individuals can expand their knowledge, gain confidence, and develop the skills necessary to navigate the ever-changing investment landscape. Remember, investing in education is an investment in yourself and your financial future.

Books and Publications on Investing: Knowledge for Financial Growth

Books and publications play a pivotal role in providing valuable insights, strategies, and knowledge about investing. They offer a wealth of information from industry experts, successful investors, and financial thought leaders.

Importance of Books and Publications on Investing:

a. In-Depth Knowledge: Books and publications delve into various investment topics, offering comprehensive and detailed information on investment strategies, market analysis, risk management, and personal finance.

b. Expert Perspectives: Many renowned investors, economists, and financial experts share their experiences, insights, and strategies through books and publications, allowing readers to benefit from their wisdom and expertise.

c. Historical Context: Books on investing often provide historical context, helping investors understand past market cycles, economic trends, and lessons learned from significant events, which can inform decision-making in the present.

d. Self-Paced Learning: Books offer the flexibility of self-paced learning, allowing readers to absorb information at their own speed, revisit chapters, and take time to reflect on concepts and strategies.

Notable Books on Investing:

a. "The Intelligent Investor" by Benjamin Graham: Considered a timeless classic, this book focuses on value investing principles and provides insights into stock selection, risk management, and long-term investing.

b. "A Random Walk Down Wall Street" by Burton Malkiel: This book explores the efficient market hypothesis and advocates for passive investing through index funds. It covers various investment vehicles, asset allocation, and investment strategies.

c. "Common Stocks and Uncommon Profits" by Philip Fisher:

Fisher shares his approach to evaluating and selecting growth stocks, emphasizing the importance of understanding a company's fundamentals and long-term prospects.

d. "The Little Book of Common Sense Investing" by John C. Bogle: Bogle, the founder of Vanguard Group, emphasizes the benefits of low-cost index fund investing and highlights the pitfalls of active management and high fees.

e. "Reminiscences of a Stock Operator" by Edwin Lefèvre: This fictionalized biography provides insights into the mindset and psychology of a successful trader, highlighting the importance of managing emotions and discipline in investing.

f. "Thinking, Fast and Slow" by Daniel Kahneman: Although not specifically about investing, this book explores the cognitive biases that influence decision-making, providing valuable insights for investors to make rational choices.

g. "The Four Pillars of Investing" by William Bernstein: This book emphasizes the core principles of asset allocation, diversification, risk management, and investor behavior, providing a holistic approach to long-term investment success.

Other Valuable Publications:

a. Financial Magazines: Magazines like Forbes, Barron's, and Money provide timely market analysis, investment insights, and articles on personal finance, helping investors stay informed about current trends and opportunities.

b. Investment Journals and Research Reports: Academic journals and research reports, such as those published by leading financial institutions and research firms, offer in-depth analysis, studies, and investment recommendations backed by extensive research.

c. Blogs and Online Publications: Numerous investment-focused blogs and online publications provide a wealth of information, market commentary, and insights from industry experts and experienced investors.

Utilizing Books and Publications:

a. Reading Strategy: Develop a reading strategy that covers a range of investment topics, including fundamental analysis, technical analysis, behavioral finance, and personal finance. Mix timeless classics with more contemporary publications to gain a well-rounded perspective.

b. Take Notes and Reflect: While reading, take notes, highlight key points, and reflect on how the concepts and strategies discussed align with your investment goals and risk tolerance. Consider how you can apply the knowledge to your own investment approach.

c. Continuous Learning: Make reading a habit and allocate dedicated time for learning and expanding your knowledge about investing. Stay updated with new releases, follow industry trends, and explore different viewpoints to deepen your understanding.

Books and publications on investing offer a treasure trove of knowledge, strategies, and insights from industry experts and successful investors. By immersing yourself in these valuable resources, you can gain a solid foundation of investment principles, understand different strategies, and develop the skills necessary to make informed investment decisions. Remember, reading is a continuous journey of learning, and incorporating books and publications into your investment education can significantly contribute to your financial growth.

Recap of Key Investment Principles

Investing can be a powerful tool to secure their financial future and achieve their long-term goals. To summarize the key investment principles that are relevant to this generation, we can highlight the following:

Start Early: Time is one of the greatest advantages for investors. Starting early allows for the power of compounding to work in their favor, potentially maximizing investment returns over the long term.

Long-Term Perspective: Embrace a long-term mindset when it comes to investing. The stock market and other asset classes may experience short-term volatility, but historical trends have shown that long-term investments tend to generate favorable returns. Avoid making hasty decisions based on short-term market fluctuations.

Diversification: Diversify your investment portfolio across different asset classes, such as stocks, bonds, real estate, and alternative investments. Diversification helps spread risk and can enhance the stability of your overall portfolio.

Asset Allocation: Determine an appropriate asset allocation that aligns with your financial goals, risk tolerance, and time horizon. Allocate your investments across different asset classes based on your investment objectives and adjust the allocation as needed over time.

Regular Portfolio Review and Rebalancing: Regularly review your portfolio to ensure it remains aligned with your goals and risk tolerance. Rebalance your portfolio periodically to maintain the desired asset allocation, selling assets that have exceeded their target percentage and investing in those that have fallen below.

Investment Costs and Fees: Be mindful of investment costs and fees, as they can erode your returns over time. Compare fees across investment platforms and consider low-cost investment options such as index funds and ETFs.

Risk Management: Understand and manage investment risks. Consider your risk tolerance and invest accordingly. Diversification, asset allocation, and periodic portfolio reviews can help mitigate risk.

Investment Education: Continuously educate yourself about investing. Read books, publications, and online resources to expand your knowledge. Consider investment courses, seminars, and workshops to enhance your understanding and skills.

Emotion Management: Avoid making investment decisions based solely on emotions or short-term market fluctuations. Stay disciplined and stick to your long-term investment strategy. Managing emotions during market volatility is key to making rational decisions.

Seek Professional Advice: Consider consulting a financial advisor who understands your specific needs and can provide personalized guidance. A financial advisor can help you navigate complex investment decisions, develop a comprehensive financial plan, and address any concerns you may have.

By adhering to these key investment principles, investors can make informed and strategic investment decisions, increase their chances of achieving their financial goals, and build a secure future for themselves and their families.

The Importance of Ongoing Education and Adaptation in the Investment World

In the fast-paced and ever-changing investment world, ongoing education and adaptation are essential for success. It is important to continuously learn, stay informed, and adapt to evolving market conditions.

The Benefits of Ongoing Education:

a. Knowledge Expansion: Ongoing education enhances your understanding of investment principles, strategies, and market dynamics. It equips you with the knowledge to make informed decisions and navigate changing market conditions.

b. Risk Mitigation: Staying educated helps identify and mitigate risks associated with investments. It enables you to recognize potential pitfalls, understand the impact of economic factors, and make prudent investment choices.

c. Improved Decision-Making: Ongoing education enhances your ability to analyze investment opportunities, evaluate risks and returns, and make well-informed decisions. It helps you develop a rational and disciplined approach to investing.

d. Adaptability: Continuous learning enables you to adapt to new investment trends, technologies, and regulations. It empowers you to adjust your strategies and seize emerging opportunities while managing potential challenges.

Strategies for Ongoing Education:

a. Read Widely: Stay updated by reading books, articles, and publications on investing. Explore a variety of sources to gain diverse perspectives and insights.

b. Attend Seminars and Workshops: Participate in investment seminars, workshops, and webinars to learn from industry experts, gain practical knowledge, and stay abreast of current trends.

c. Online Courses and Certifications: Enroll in online courses and certifications specific to investing and finance. These courses offer structured learning and provide in-depth knowledge on various investment topics.

d. Join Investment Communities: Engage with investment communities, both online and offline, to exchange ideas, discuss investment strategies, and learn from experienced investors.

e. Follow Financial News: Stay informed about market trends, economic indicators, and company news through financial news outlets, podcasts, and investment newsletters.

Adapting Investment Strategies:

a. Monitor Market Conditions: Regularly assess market conditions and economic trends that may impact your investments. Keep an eye on interest rates, geopolitical events, regulatory changes, and industry disruptions.

b. Review and Adjust Portfolio: Periodically review your investment portfolio to ensure it remains aligned with your goals, risk tolerance, and market conditions. Make adjustments as needed to optimize your asset allocation and diversification.

c. Embrace Technological Advancements: Leverage technological tools and platforms to streamline investment processes, access real-time data, and utilize advanced analytics for better decision-making.

d. Seek Professional Guidance: Consider consulting with financial advisors or investment professionals who can provide expert guidance, especially during times of market uncertainty or when complex investment decisions arise.

The Psychology of Adaptation:

a. Overcome Confirmation Bias: Avoid clinging to preconceived notions or being overly influenced by existing beliefs. Stay open-minded and adapt your investment strategies based on objective analysis and new information.

b. Embrace Flexibility: Be willing to modify your investment approach as market conditions evolve. Flexibility allows you to seize opportunities and adjust strategies to changing circumstances.

c. Manage Emotions: Emotional discipline is critical in the investment world. Develop strategies to manage fear, greed, and impulsive decision-making. Stay focused on long-term goals and avoid making rash decisions based on short-term market fluctuations.

In the dynamic world of investing, ongoing education and adaptation are key to achieving long-term success. By continuously expanding your knowledge, staying informed, and adapting your investment strategies, you can navigate changing market conditions, manage risks, and seize new opportunities. Embrace the mindset of a lifelong learner, be open to evolving trends and technologies, and strive to improve your investment decision-making abilities. Through ongoing education and adaptation, you'll position yourself for success in the ever-evolving investment landscape.

SUMMARY

I sincerely hope your head isn't spinning right now. Investing is important if you want to grow your wealth. I've recently encountered a few individuals who were so afraid of investing – of any kind – that they decided to keep their money safely deposited in their local bank. This is all well and good now that interest rates have finally begun to increase, but for a while, they were near zero, which means you were earning next to nothing in your money.

Look at investing legends such as Warren Buffett. He is now considered a genius but at one time he was in the same boat as you and I. Buffett wasn't born into wealth. He learned how to invest and is now referred to as one of the greatest investors of all time. Buffett implemented a value-based strategy for much of his career, meaning he only invested in companies that earn money, pay dividends or are a bit safer than some of the high-risk names – meme stocks – we hear about when we read about people getting rich quickly.

Investing is a long-term game. You don't hear about long-term success stories very often. All you ever hear about is how the woman won the lottery or how that man invested $1,000 in

Bitcoin 10 years ago and is now a millionaire. Yes, these stories are real. These people do exist, but they either got lucky, timed the market perfectly (which may only happen a few times in life), or were just in the right place at the right time.

I urge you to visit this book every few months or so and evaluate your investing life. This isn't a one-and-done thing. Investing needs to evolve over your lifetime just as your life itself will evolve. Overall, this comprehensive guide aims to empower investors with the knowledge, strategies, and confidence to navigate the world of investing and build a secure financial future. It emphasizes the importance of ongoing education, adaptability, and taking action while providing practical insights and tips for successful investing.

I will leave you with one of Warren Buffett's most famous quotes: "The first rule of investing is don't lose money. And the second rule of investing is don't forget the first rule. And that's all the rules there are."

Happy Investing!